Sex, God, and Rock 'n' Roll

Sex, God, and Rock 'n' Roll

Catastrophes, Epiphanies, and Sacred Anarchies

Barry Taylor

Fortress Press

Minneapolis

SEX, GOD, AND ROCK 'N' ROLL
Catastrophes, Epiphanies, and Sacred Anarchies

Cover image: javarman3/iStock
Cover design: Alisha Lofgren

Print ISBN: 978-1-5064-0906-1
eBook ISBN: 978-1-5064-0907-8

Dedication:

M. The end. Done.

Acknowledgment:

Memory is imagined.

Contents

Foreword   xiii
Pete Rollins

Introduction   xvi

PART I. SEX: THE BIOLOGICAL

1.   Comfort   3

2.   Where Dreams Go to Die   8

3.   To Be Invisible   14

4.   Under the Waves   16

5.   My Younger Self   20

6.   The Drip-Feed of Erotic Data   23

7.   Thoughts on Death   28

8.   A Theology of Kissing   34

PART II. DRUGS: THE EXPERIENTIAL

9.   A Box I've Never Opened   43

10.   Play Fucking Loud   45

11.	Migraines and Melancholy (Or Knowing One's Darkness)	48
12.	Creative Chaos	52
13.	Dressing the Sacred	56
14.	Dirt	61
15.	Skulls	64
16.	Capitalism on Drugs (Or Our Love Affair with Non-Permanent Pharmacological Lobotomies)	67
17.	My Own Judas	72
18.	Tattoos	75
19.	Love Is a Losing Game	80
20.	The Sound of Failure	82
21.	Shoes	85
22.	When Tokyo Was Still the Future: Why I Travel	87
23.	Orvieto	91

PART III. ART: THE CREATIVE

24.	I Missed Punk, but I Got the Message	97
25.	Collage, Bricolage, Assemblage	105
26.	Elvis's Belly	109
27.	Fallen Angels	112
28.	An Elegy for Leonard Cohen	114
29.	When Is a Painting Not a Painting?	116

30.	Twombly	123
31.	Bowie and Me	125

PART IV. RELIGION: THE SPIRITUAL

32.	The Other Woman	135
33.	A Theological Life	143
34.	On Smugness	145
35.	A Shout	147
36.	Between Carnival and Lent	150
37.	Dead Gods	155
38.	Hello, Darkness	162
39.	Losing Jesus	166
40.	Notes on the Death of God	175
41.	Religion and a Rabbit's Foot	178
42.	Apocalypse Will Blossom	181

Foreword

Pete Rollins

It is generally believed that the journey toward the universal requires walking a wide path. In the natural sciences, a single result that appears to prove a theory could well be an anomaly. Tests have to be repeated, new experiments devised.

Only when a theory is verified repeatedly does it begin to take the shape of knowledge. Similarly, in psychology, larger sample sizes mean more trustworthy results. The more people in an experiment, the more you can minimize individual eccentricities and glimpse general principles.

But philosophers such as Søren Kierkegaard understood that some of the deepest insights don't arise from large sample sizes and generalized tests. Rather, they surface from a deep penetration of the singular. By courageously digging as deep as possible into his own subjectivity, Kierkegaard wrote in a way that revealed something about the nature of human existence. He wasn't unique in this approach, but his work significantly impacted how many twentieth-century philosophers approached the biggest questions.

This way of entry into knowledge marks the work of psychoanalysis. For instance, Sigmund Freud left us with only five significant case studies, which are still referenced to this day. For people such as Kierkegaard and Freud, we must take the narrow path of the singular if we want to approach the promised land of knowledge.

In this theological memoir, Barry Taylor has given us a beautiful example of this journey along the narrow path. He shares fragments of his life that are deeply personal, yet reach into the dark recesses of what it means to be.

The words *metaphysics* and *spirituality* have become trite terms today. Bookstores use them as categories to house insipid collections of new-age nonsense. These books call their inane ideas ancient wisdom and wrap basic personality tests in religious language or offer self-help through the power of positive thinking.

The words have become so distorted that one must be careful when using them. But they are important words, and they are appropriate to use in describing this work. Metaphysics can be provisionally understood as referring to questions regarding the status of what is not reducible to the field of the physical, while spirituality describes how one tarries with and makes room for this dimension. Traditionally, these questions have been the staple of theology, but we see this dimension also playing out in other fields. In biology, we have the antagonism at the heart of evolution. In mathematics, we have the uncertainty principle. In physics, we have the quantum world. In psychoanalysis, we have the unconscious. These are all descriptions of something that is *in* the world, but not of it.

This book is a work that is truly spiritual in the most earthed and authentic way. Taylor has given us a profane book on the spiritual, a non-superstitious work that touches on metaphysical questions. In doing so, he avoids the beasts of scientism and superstition, the two demonic dangers philosopher Paul Tillich told us authentic theology defends against. While one flattens out the world with a hammer, the other splits it in two with a sword.

Taylor doesn't write with a hammer or a sword. Instead, he writes in the tradition of someone like Simone Weil, helping us discern what we might call the holy dimension of reality. Not holy in the sense of something outside the world, but rather the wholly, as in a wholly other dimension within our world. One that does not commit us to belief in angels, demons, or gods any more than our confidence in the scientific method commits us to a crude materialism. Taylor is a profane priest who offers us a depth of understanding that goes beyond the tired distinctions between theist and atheist, sacred and secular.

It helps that this profane priest combines two things that rarely meet: an academically trained writer and someone who throws his arms around life. If this were only a memoir, it would be a fascinating read. And if it were a standard theological text, it would be deeply insightful. But the way the two become one within these pages makes it utterly compelling.

This is one of those rare books that has the power to offer the reader intellectual riches, while also leaving them with something that might make their own tarrying with the negative slightly less difficult. Indeed, it might even make it fun.

Introduction

Life unfolds in fragments. We spend too much time trying to piece things together to create the illusion of some overarching scheme to our existence. Life is made up of bits and pieces, routines and rituals, catastrophes and epiphanies. These mundane, everyday experiences are the relationships that form you, and the unexpected moments when the whole axis of your life shifts. We tend to think these unexpected, life-changing events will arrive with more grandeur, warning, or significance, but it can be throwaway comments, casual encounters, or unplanned, inconvenient situations that become points of departure and arrival. These are the moments when life comes into focus.

I have gathered some fragments of my life in this book. Stories, essays, ideas, and thoughts—particularly about what I call my theological life. I have lived much of my adult life in the realm of the gods, talking about, thinking about, and practicing religion. Philosopher Mark C. Taylor says religion is the most interesting where it is the least obvious. I think I know what he means: theology is what is left when everything else has been taken away. My very human existence, all of it—the moments, the shoes I wear, the religion, the sex, the art I create, the doubts that haunt me, and the moments of great revelation that guide me—this is my life.

Sigmund Freud wrote about what he called the palliatives, or the ways in which humans have attempted to ease the pain of existence: sex, drugs, art, and religion. It makes sense that these forces shaped my life the most, and so form the basis of the stories told here. The "Sex" section centers on the biological: family, life, death, and of course, sex. "Drugs" contains essays about the ephemera of life—things that stimulate, captivate, or interest. "Art" is the creative bits and pieces of life, and "Religion" is the spiritual or immaterial. It makes sense to start to with sex because, well, that's how we all begin our journey into this world. We are all accidents of birth thrown into the world by the most primal of acts, and it was a primal act that began my theological life.

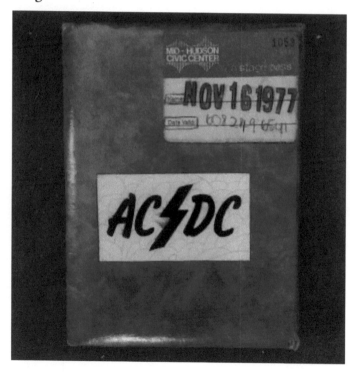

My journal from 1977

PART I

Sex: The Biological

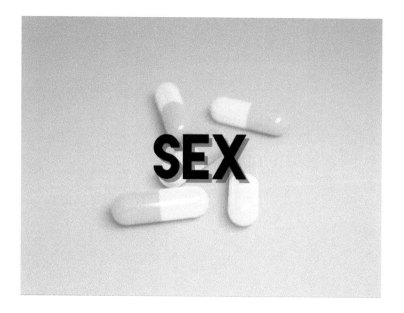

1

Comfort

Once upon a time, I was in San Antonio, Texas, in the late 1970s. The band I was working for, AC/DC, was playing at a music festival, so we stayed there for a couple days, which was not our usual modus operandi at the time. We had been criss-crossing America—well, the world, really—as the band made its mark on the world of rock 'n' roll.

I began working for the band in its early days. They had just moved to London from Australia and were looking to pick up a British crew to tour America with them. At the time, my friend Ian and I were touring the UK with the Stylistics, but the lure of an American tour was enough to get us to pack up and join them. I'd never heard their music and did not meet them until we were all on a ferry to France. Ian and I were their only crew in the beginning. We loaded the equipment in and out of gigs, controlled the sound, and managed everything else necessary to pull off a live show. We traversed the US in a truck and a rental car, the two of us and the band, truck-stopping and cheap-hoteling our way around the country. We drove hundreds of miles day and night to open for Kiss, Aerosmith, and many other bands further up the rock 'n' roll food chain at the time.

By the time we got to San Antonio, things had changed. The band had hit America at the right time, and small shows were quickly turning into big ones. The crew was expanding, and there was more equipment, more trucks, more notoriety, and a growing sense that this band was unstoppable. Every show built on the previous one. Each time we returned to a city, the venue was larger, the energy was stronger, and we had been spending more and more time on the road. AC/DC was becoming one of the biggest bands in rock.

I do not remember how I came to be by myself that night. It was late, and I think the rest of the crew had gone down to the San Antonio River Walk to unwind after the show. Touring life lacks privacy; when you live with a small group 24/7, everything you do is in full view of everyone else. Living on a tour bus, constantly surrounded by the rest of the crew, was difficult. Every once in a while, I just needed some space.

On my way back into the hotel, I bumped into a girl whom I had met there a couple times during our stay. She had caught my eye, but this was the first time I had encountered her alone. We chatted in the hallway for a bit, then she asked if I wanted to go home with her. I said yes. That's how it was then—or how it seemed to be when you were young, reckless, and on the road with a band. Sex—with strangers and people you barely knew—was part and parcel of the experience.

When we got to her place, we went directly to the bedroom. She said she didn't want to wake the "others," so we had to be quiet. She told me to get in bed and that she would be right back. I waited there, and soon she returned naked and joined me in bed. I could tell you about her beauty, the exotic thrill, or the anticipation of the encounter, but that's all a little vague. What I remember is that she got on top of me and said, "Do you mind if we pray?"

She proceeded to say a lengthy and heartfelt prayer to Jesus, one I later came to realize was a very evangelical, born-again-

Christian prayer—personal, imploring, intercessory. She prayed for me, my life, my heart, and the sex we were about to have. I was taken aback, but also curious. I'd never experienced anything like that before. I just laid there as she straddled me, eyes closed, arms uplifted. "Amen," she said. Then we fucked.

In the morning, I was gently awoken by another girl, who asked if I wanted to join everybody for breakfast. I made my way down the hall to the dining room, where I was greeted by almost a dozen people I can only describe as hippies. They had guitars and smiles, and on the table in front of them were a bunch of open Bibles. I was not sure what I had walked into, but they were all friendly and asked me about my life. Over breakfast, they told me they all loved Jesus and that they lived together as one big family. They sang several happy songs, and soon the Jesus talk got a little intense. I remember feeling relieved that I had to get back to the hotel because we were leaving that morning for our next gig.

I wouldn't discover until much later that the girl I had sex with was part of a cult called the Children of God. It was one of the many fringe groups that emerged in the late 1970s as spirituality made its return into the landscape of youth culture. Out of the counterculture all kinds of communes and communities—religious and otherwise—emerged, and her group was just one of them. Groups of varying religious perspectives materialized around the globe as the post-hippie generation began reframing its views on life and the beyond. Jesus was in the mix—radically redefined, but present nonetheless. The women in the Children of God practiced a unique form of evangelism by offering sex in attempt to gain new members. The woman I had slept with was named Comfort—I don't know if that was her real name or if her cult gave people new names, but given her warmth toward me, it was perfect for her. I never saw her again.

Nothing particularly profound happened to me that night. I

had sex with a girl I barely knew. I did not have a transcendent experience, find God, or become reborn. I wasn't looking for any of that, but I *had* been thinking deeply about where my life was headed, and I had hunger for a deeper, richer, more meaningful life. See, that night in San Antonio was the first encounter I'd had with religion as an adult. It was the first time a peer had invoked a religious figure in a meaningful way, and it was the first time Jesus floated into my world when I was a young man. It was a strange encounter, sure, but we should never underestimate how things might float into our lives.

So, what do you do after an encounter like that? You do what I did: when you get to your next stop in Nashville, you buy a Bible.

A Brief Epilogue

A while ago, I was interviewed by Rob Bell on his podcast, *The RobCast*. For the first time publicly, I talked about that encounter. A couple weeks after the episode aired, I received a message from someone who claimed to be the daughter of a woman who once lived in San Antonio and was a member of the Children of God. Apparently, some former members had listened to the episode and passed it around to their friends. The daughter's message was sweet and kind; she had enjoyed the things I spoke about. She told me that her mother, who now lived in Mexico, had heard the episode too and wanted me to know that she still loved Jesus. She said her mother's name was Comfort, the only person named Comfort from San Antonio any of the former members could remember.

I have carried this story inside me for decades, and I have not had the language necessary to tell it before now. It is an important story to me because it was a catalyst in my journey toward something I never imagined for myself: a theological life. My journey in, through, and out of a particular Christianity had no room in its vocabulary for telling the tale the way it needed to be told. Now I have the words, as well as awareness that strange and profane moments like this, which don't necessarily fit into the formula of how things are supposed to work, have been vital in the paths my life has taken. These events shattered my notions of coherence and consistency in my world and alerted me to the random magic and mystery of life. They made space for chance, experimentation, and possibilities I never knew were there.

2

Where Dreams Go to Die

They fuck you up, your mum and dad / They don't mean to, but they do.

—Phillip Larkin

The philosopher Paul Ricoeur used to ask a question of all who attended his seminars: "*D'où parlez-vous?*" Where do you speak from? It's an important question; none of us exist in a vacuum. What we say and do is often shaped by where we are from, geographically, philosophically, socially. We are all accidents of birth, as my friend Jack Caputo, another philosopher, is fond of saying. We do not get to choose where we are thrown into the world, but where we land goes a long way toward shaping the rest of our lives. The place to which I was thrown—a working-class county town in England—continues to influence my life.

I was born in a town called Woking in Surrey, close to London. When I was about eight, we left Woking for Huntingdon, my father's hometown, and I spent my most of my formative years there. Huntingdon used to be a county town, meaning it had a certain position and charm. It was a thriving center of the local farming economy, with regular markets drawing farmers in from surrounding towns and villages.

Also a place of history, Huntingdon was the birthplace of

Oliver Cromwell: the Lord Protector of England, a Puritan leader, and part of the army that forced Charles I from his throne and established a new form of government. Huntingdon was also allegedly connected to Robin Hood, but Cromwell is enough notoriety for a small town. I have said more than once that I grew up in an area of Britain known for dissenters and nontraditionalists, so if troublemaking and rabble-rousing is indeed in my bones, it comes from the soil of my father's side of the family.

But by the time we moved to Huntingdon, things had changed dramatically. The town had become a faded glory and was now characterized by a ring of housing estates built in the 1950s and '60s to resettle Londoners after World War II. It was called an overflow town. The new housing estates had been tacked on to the edge of town, then a ring road was built around the old town to connect them. The estates were uniform and bleak. New but architecturally uninspiring little boxes, they were all about functionality. Warren-like alleys separated the houses, and little streets trickled into the old town. The whole place felt disconnected, and a sense of alienation hovered over it. The town had also been turned into a netherworld—there weren't enough jobs, and the old townspeople suspected the new "outsiders" had brought big-city trouble with them. None of that was true, but it colored the perspective of life in Huntingdon.

We were a working-class family. Our lives were not grim, and we had what we needed, but little more. As I grew older, this caused me a lot of shame. To be honest, I like the working-class notions I grew up with. There is something noble about the idea of honest, hard-working life. The shame comes from much closer to home. It wasn't being working class that caused it, but rather my personal family experience of it. My home life was marked by an almost painful silence and passivity, as well as a pathological lack of ambition. There is an attitude common to

Britain's working classes, particularly of my father's generation and before, that manifests in things such as making the best of what little you have and taking pride in your place in society. My father didn't wear his working-class status with any sense of pride, but he operated on a particular iteration of it: "Accept your lot in life. There is no room for you anywhere but at the bottom the pile, so why try do anything about it?" Unlike me, he found little nobility in being a working man. He wasn't bitter, just resigned. I think there was a time when this attitude about being working class was more pervasive, but by the time I came of age, the whole class structure of British society had been rattled by the emergence of postwar youth culture. Ideas about aspirational living and changing one's circumstances had become part of the fabric of many people's lives in the working class, but somehow it missed my house—or at least my father.

He spent his whole life digging holes in the road for a local gas company, and even in that job his lack of ambition kept him at the lowest level. It always felt like he had assigned himself some kind of personal penance. He never tried to climb in his working life, even though he could have. That deep-seated resignation shaped him, and it has nipped at my heels my whole life as a consequence. I find myself easily falling into the trap that the hard way must be the only way, and I should be punished for wanting anything more. I live thousands of miles away from that life—in fact, I ran here as fast and as early as I could—but that message still haunts me.

I Grew Up in the Home Where Dreams Went to Die

G. K. Chesterton in his book *Heretics* wrote that when we step into a family, we step into a world that has its "own strange laws, a world we have not made." He says we step into a fairy tale when we step into a family. I don't agree that it's always a fairy tale; sometimes it's a horror story. Perhaps they are the same thing, if we see fairy tales for what they are: slightly twisted and sometimes cruel inversions of reality that offer lessons about life.

My father wore his poverty with nonchalance. Not so much with a carefree attitude, but with more of a disregard. He had few friends and spent his time off mostly alone, and he seldom expressed joy. I can still conjure up an image of my mother laughing, but I have no such recall of my father. He wasn't grumpy, but whatever happiness or joy he experienced, he kept it firmly under wraps. Our family had no car, no washing machine, and no refrigerator. We had an old black-and-white television and hand-me-down furniture. Any of this he seemed not to notice. All around us, other working families were slowly making their lives more comfortable and middle class, but it went right by him. He seemed to derive no pleasure from life, so his lack of means posed no threat. His needs were simple. He went to the pub Saturday and Sunday mornings for a couple hours, always alone. He was a man passing through life who wanted nothing more than to be left alone.

He and my mother lived separate social lives. She had friends, but he did not seem to need them. His brother lived about a mile away from us, but we rarely visited him. My father also had a sister, whom I had never heard of until I was in my forties. My mother's relationship with her family was not much better; she came from a family of nine children, but I barely saw my uncles and aunts. Her family was laden with troubling secrets that still occasionally surface.

Don't get me wrong: we always had food, heat, and clothing. Our poverty was largely emotional. We didn't have any money, but that wasn't the real issue. What we lacked—what *I* lacked—was attention, care, input, and stimulation. Neither of my parents gave much of a shit about anything to do with my life, or my brother's, for that matter. We were often left to our own devices. My friends thought my parents' lack of control was liberating because I could do whatever I wanted, but I yearned for direction and guidance—even if it was limiting. They never came to my school events, and they seldom commented on anything I did. I just did my own thing.

My dad was brooding, occasionally acerbic, and generally silent. He barely spoke to anyone, including my mom. My childhood memories are of the four of us sitting in our tiny dining room at night with the television on and nobody speaking except to ask if anyone wanted tea. At my father's funeral, people who had known him his whole life commented on his silence and noted that he barely, if ever, acknowledged anyone.

I had two significant conversations with my father. The first was when I got arrested for drug possession. I was still in school then, and had spent a Friday night in jail. I got home around lunchtime to find him watching wrestling on television. I stood in front of the television to get his attention. When I told him what had happened, he said, "Don't do that again. You'll upset your mother. Now, let me watch the wrestling." I felt conflicted: part of me was relieved that he didn't punish me, but the other part could not shake the feeling that to him I counted for nothing, and that nothing I could do—good or bad—would get his attention. So, I left and went to drop acid with a friend.

The second conversation was years later, about a week before he died. He had been diagnosed with cancer that came on quickly, and he died within about three months. Our conversation again took place in front of the television, but it was a horse race this time. He was a shadow of himself now, his life ebbing away. He sat in his usual chair like an African chieftain: upright, one hand holding his walking stick and the other on his chin, where it always was. We had no idea what he wanted with regard to his funeral, and my mom was too upset to talk to him about it, so I said I would do it. It is never a conversation you want to have, but there I was, trying to get him to focus, not on me this time but on himself.

"So, Dad, we know it won't be long now," I said. "Is there

anything you want to talk about? Do you have any preferences about your funeral? Do you want a church service? Tell us what you'd like because we don't know."

I tried my best to be forthright and honest, hoping this conversation would be unlike any other I'd had with him. The stakes were higher now. Even though nobody had said anything out loud, we all knew death was stalking the heart of our family. It had made its way into our midst and our family unit would never be the same. But what I got from him was the same stoic resignation I had always received. The reality of his death had not changed him.

He did not flinch when he got his diagnosis. There were no tears, at least not in our presence. He exhibited no sense of anguish or confusion. He was not about to fight his cancer. He had just accepted it as another inevitable part of his lot in life. I don't know if he had an inner dialogue I wasn't privy to, but I'd like to think he did. Part of me thought it was somewhat heroic for him to be so unmoved, but the other part of me felt the loss for him, for us all.

"I don't care," he said. "Put me in a box, burn me, and throw the ashes away. It doesn't matter. I won't be here anyway."

That was it. He didn't want a church funeral. He didn't want music, a eulogy, or a Scripture reading. He just wanted to be burned and discarded, end of conversation. He drifted back to the horse race, and a week or so later he drifted out of this world, with my mom out of the room and my brother and me sitting on the bed, watching the old man die.

3

To Be Invisible

Taylor family

Nobody in my family likes having their picture taken. It must seem strange in our world of selfies, overexposure, and self-confidence, but fear of the camera is one characteristic every member of my family shares. It is as though my entire family wants to be invisible. I bet there aren't more than twenty pictures of my family together from my entire upbringing. This photo sums us up. It was taken without warning, and this was our collective reaction.

As for the spoons on the wall, my dad collected them. They were novelty spoons of vistas all over the world, mostly given to him by others. He seldom traveled and we never went on family holidays. If he wasn't working, he would spend time in his garden. The thought of going somewhere? Anathema. But somewhere underneath whatever it was that stifled him, he held an awareness and a curiosity about the world. I picked up that spirit and have been running with it since I was able.

I felt responsible for the lack of attention I received from my parents, that somehow I made them ignore me the way they did. I grew up wondering if I counted for anything, because I never got the idea that my parents cared very much. I have offered many excuses for them—they were both hardworking, we were left to our own devices because they were in subsistence mode, they didn't have time for niceties, etc. The problem is that I had other friends whose family lives and economic challenges were as restricted as ours, and their experiences were much different. I am not mad about this, but it did fuck me up a bit. I am still haunted by the ghosts that were handed to me when I came into his world.

Some fucking fairy tale, Chesterton. Some fairly tale.

4

Under the Waves

Simon Critchley, a philosopher, says we discover what our relationship with our mother is like when our fathers are no longer in the picture. I'm sure his philosophy is linked to some Freudian notion about fathers and sons wrestling for the love of the mother, all very Oedipal. I don't know what I think about that, but my relationship with my mom has been every bit as conflicted as my relationship with my father.

Once, my parents and I went to Hawaii together. On our first morning, I suggested a drive around the island, but my mother wanted to go swimming. So, off we all went, beyond pale British people, down to the gorgeous edge of the Pacific Ocean. My mom couldn't wait to swim; I'd never seen her so lighthearted and giddy, like a child. She'd spent a year preparing for this moment by learning to swim at her local public pool. As my dad hid in the shadows of a covered lounge chair, my mother threw down her stuff and aimed straight for the water.

"Hold on, mom. I'll come with you," I said.

"Don't worry about me," she replied. "I'll be just fine."

I watched her go down to the water with a boldness I had never seen and she waded straight out. I'd never seen her in a swimsuit, let alone swim, and I thought she seemed a little unprepared for the strength of the ocean. After all, a swimming pool in England is a far cry from the Pacific Ocean. She didn't make it very far out before I could see her struggling, disappearing under the waves only to reappear seconds later and flap around confusedly. I jumped in and swam out to her. She was in trouble, and it took a minute or two to get her sorted out and back toward the shore.

She was scared and flustered. "I couldn't feel the bottom," she said. "I couldn't feel the bottom!" Suddenly, I realized that the whole time my mom had been learning to swim, she had kept one leg touching the ground and hadn't really learned to swim at all. She knew how to make the motions of swimming, but she had spent that whole time bouncing along with her foot pressing on the bottom of the pool. She never swam again, and we never spoke of it any time that holiday was mentioned.

My mother is now ravaged by dementia. She is losing words and comprehension, tormented by a form of the disease that comes with voices and visions. She has not known who I am for over a year now, which is strange, as this is the person who birthed me into the world. At the same time it is apropos, because I feel like we never really knew each other. Sometimes she looks right through me, knowing that she ought to recognize me, or at least doing so only vaguely. But again, this feels familiar—when I was a child, she always looked right through me, as if she did not know what to do or say to me.

The reasons for this are complex and unclear. It may have to do with her illness at my birth and the strange way we both began our life journey together. She contracted spinal meningitis and was in the hospital and very ill for the first eight months or so of my life. We were connected by blood but separated by sickness in those formative months of my life. I tried therapy for a while to see if I could bridge the chasm between us, but it takes two to tango and she never seemed game to try. Every time I suggested we needed to address these issues between us, she quickly lowered a wall of indignation and defiance. Perhaps the discomfort of facing the reality of our lack of connection made her push it, and me, away. In the thirty years I've lived in America, she's called me less than a handful of times.

I think at one point I was trying to replace my mother in other relationships, to find elsewhere what I missed in her. But I don't want to be mothered by anyone else and I've long since stopped looking. That sounds insensitive and uncaring, but I can only say it is how I feel. I have affection and warmth for my mother and father for who they are, but I am deeply conflicted about where to put all the things I feel about my upbringing. There was a time when I was angry about it all, wracked by insecurity and questioning why they bothered having kids if they were so disinclined to care.

My biggest challenge growing up was lacking a model for love, not only how to love but how to *be* loved. Love has been difficult for me. I have been loved much and I have loved in return, but I have a deep restlessness that goes way, way back. When it rises to the surface, things can go wrong rapidly.

I am still haunted by the many ghosts I inherited from my family. I still battle the same things: insecurity, self-loathing, self-hatred, self-destruction, being the invisible man, and a very loud and critical voice inside me that is seldom drowned out by other voices or opinions. I got out as quickly as I could by any means necessary. Music was my first refuge, but then came drugs. I used them to escape, altering my consciousness to deal with what I had no capacity to handle any other way. And then I escaped with geography—I moved to Europe with friends, then went on the road with bands. Finally, I moved to America. Anywhere was better than home.

Me squashed in the crowd, somewhere in America late '70s

5

My Younger Self

A couple years ago, I was browsing in a bookstore when I stumbled upon a book about AC/DC. Thumbing through it, I happened upon a picture of me that I have in one of my own old albums. In it, I'm behind Angus Young, AC/DC's lead guitarist, who is sitting on the shoulders of singer Bon Scott. We were in the middle of a huge arena in Oakland, California. I was there to make sure the crowd didn't pull Angus to the ground. This was part of the band's concert ritual—Angus would play while riding right into the middle of the crowd on Bon's shoulders. They would break the wall between performer and audience, and they were one of the few bands that attempted that kind of thing. In the early days before wireless guitar technology, it was a nightmare to keep two musicians plus a ridiculously long guitar cable from the audience, so a few of us would have to dive into the crowd with them and try to hold back the manic fans desperate to touch the hem of their idol's garments. It was always a mad scene, wading into thousands of rabid fans. In the photo, I'm barely holding on, almost drowning in a sea of humanity.

I was probably twenty-two at the time, back in the giddy days when the band was conquering America and the shows were insane everywhere we went. As I stood there in the bookshop looking at that picture of a barely recognizable me, I realized I had been given an opportunity to address my younger self. What would I say to him?

Pretty mundane and expected things, I think. Essentially, all the things I have struggled with most of my life:

- Don't settle.

- Trust your gut.

- Find your voice as early as you can. Say what you want and mean what you say.

- Care for your friends. You'll need them and they mean more than you know. Some of them can't be replaced.

- Love is worth the trouble. Sex is too.

- You'll become familiar with your own ghosts and you'll be surprised at how resilient they are.

- Don't believe in quick fixes, because there generally aren't.

- You really should have told that girl you loved her, because you did. You just overthought it.

I'd also tell him that life is a struggle and there are no easy answers. Maybe life has no meaning at all other than the living of it, and he could relax a little on the existential angst.

I'd tell him there will be moments of sublime, breathtaking beauty and times of unspeakable pain and loss. He already knows this, but it's good to remind him.

I'd tell him that, above all, his restless internal struggle will not go away. He should nurture the gifts that came with it: insatiable curiosity, a desire to learn, and a hunger for passionate engagement with the world and people around him.

Of course, maybe my younger self has a few things to say to me about not letting go of dreams or not settling for less. He might say I should deal with that crippling self-loathing, so I don't destroy myself. He might point me back to earlier times when I was more brazen and adventurous, and admonish me for the times I sacrificed doing what I wanted and being who I needed to be because I was afraid others wouldn't like it.

He would probably raise his voice on that one. And he should.

6

The Drip-Feed of Erotic Data

Traveling with a rock band will do wonders for your sex life. For a while, the sex, drugs, and rock 'n' roll life made it easy for me. The heavy-lifting of finding people and dating was removed by time constraints and by my close association with fame and celebrity, which is a surprisingly effective aphrodisiac. The funny thing about sex in an environment like that is how quickly it can become rote and formulaic. You meet some girl—well, you encounter each other, you both know why you're there, and any pretense of a long-term relationship is thrown out the window. It's just a temporary physical encounter, some more intense than others. Maybe that sounds great, and let me tell you, it is—but there's also a dark side to it.

20,000 Days on Earth, the documentary about singer Nick Cave, frequently features him ruminating on various aspects of his life. In one, he speaks of the "drip-feed of erotic data," or the early images and encounters that shaped his sexual life. Where does sexual desire begin? What makes us interested in this person rather than another? Why does the sight of one person's body arouse us while a million others could walk by naked and we would be unmoved? I have no idea, but I can say I have been on a drip-feed of erotic data for a few decades now.

I came of age in the wake of the 1960s sexual revolution. There was an excitement about it—long-standing norms had changed, and it felt like the whole world had shifted. But not everything.

My parents used to read the *Sun*, one of Britain's big tabloids that was big on celebrity scandals and short on real reporting. Any political news was essentially reduced to a witty slogan in order to keep the masses entertained, scandalized, and woefully uninformed. But the *Sun*'s real selling point for many years was the Page Three girl. Every day there would be a photo of some buxom, semi-naked girl from somewhere in mid-England. She would be splashed topless across an entire page every morning. Maybe the drip-feed began there.

In classic and predictable form, this was also the time when I stumbled upon my dad's porn collection. Well, it was more just a few magazines stacked beneath his bedside table, mainly nudist magazines and an occasional *Playboy*. That transgressive exploration of prohibited adult material fueled my desire. The desire was already there, but these images channeled it into a patchwork quilt formed of clumsy childhood discoveries.

The pop culture of my upbringing added to data as well. The Page Three and *Playboy* girls were soon joined by Brigitte Bardot, Jane Birkin, Jane Fonda, Joan Jett, Madonna, Suzi Quatro, and Charlotte Rampling. These avalanches of images came from everywhere, from the writings of D. H. Lawrence to Anaïs Nin to Japanese hentai. There were stockings, tattoos, bondage wear, fetishes. Once, my best friend's girlfriend posed for a spread in a magazine called *Mayfair*; when we all celebrated at the pub, they called her Elvira the Witch. All these images floated in the cultural ether, shaping my sexual curiosity and nurturing my drives and desires.

Talking about sex is complicated, a clash of social norms and morals with stark carnal realities. It becomes even more difficult when you factor in religion. Much of my adult life, and therefore my sexual life, has been lived out under the influence of religious opining, most of it unhelpful and naïve. I've met many people who have been messed up sexually because of things they were told about sex through their religious environs. I don't want to condemn religion wholesale for its opinions, but when it comes to sex and sexuality, the conversation is often little more than prohibition and demonization.

Sins of the flesh carry lots of currency. This stretches back to old views about dualism, prioritizing the ineffable over the material. We act surprised when someone violates a taboo and acts out of impulse, or out of a resistance to the status quo. In my late teens or early twenties, some friends and I visited a drag bar called Scaramouche in a nearby town. We were all curious about pushing our limits, those internal and those handed down to us. We were drawn to the bar's taboo and illicit nature. The hint of scandal boosted the boring world we lived in. I never crossed the line from voyeurism to participation, out of fear and hesitation more than anything. That experience taught me early on that human sexuality is complex. Desire takes many forms, and while we create norms and operate within general parameters for most of our sexual lives, there are many deviating paths to choose from.

Religion is all about bodies. When our sexual lives come into contact with God, what happens? Are they compromised or intensified? A theology of sexuality, of flesh, of carnality is a theology of life itself, of life and death. The Italian philosopher Giorgio Agamben, in his 2009 book *Nudities*, writes that nudity has a theological signature in our culture, related to the story of Adam and Eve, who were naked and unashamed but had to be covered after the fall. Agamben links Western views on nudity, dress, and shame to that formative story of human brokenness and our attempts to cover up the vulnerability revealed by the actions taken in the Garden of Eden. A culture not raised on that tale of nakedness and shame might find itself with an entirely different view on the same issues.

Obsession with sex—or with particular views on sexuality and gender—seems to be one of the downfalls of the modern church. Its moral crusading against various forms of sexual encounters have only added to the disaffection many feel for Christianity. What's the answer?

Maybe we should move away from prognosticating about sexual acts and begin again with love. Of course, no one knows love better than French philosophers. Alain Badiou suggests in *In Praise of Love* that any and all sexual encounters are ultimately an encounter with ourselves. "Sex separates," he says; in the sexual act we are "in relationship with ourselves through another." Badiou says focusing on love rather than sex might lead to a different understanding of the intersections of desire, and further deepen our experience of sex and love. Desire fetishizes the other partner, especially their physical attributes, but as Badiou says, "love focuses on the very being of the other, on the other as it has erupted, fully armed with its being, into my life that is consequently disrupted and re-fashioned."

I write this in the heat of the #MeToo movement. Women and men across the globe have taken to social media to tell their stories of surviving sexual misconduct, abuse, and trauma, often inflicted by powerful men in politics, arts, religion, literature, or film. Numerous scandals have erupted as these accusations work their way through our social and political fabric. The list of toxic things that have gone undealt with for decades— sex, power, misogyny, manipulation, and more—grows longer every day.

Some say the sexual revolution of the 1960s is responsible for all of this. I am not so sure. The answer is not more conservative views about sex, but more radical ones. The sexual revolution attempted to liberate sex and sexuality from its prior strictures and boundaries. Things changed certainly, but like many of the revolutionary ideas that permeated the counterculture, they never fully took hold. #MeToo shows the need for a radical rethinking of sexuality. Old binaries and male-driven power dynamics are hopelessly and dangerously outmoded. As notions about power, gender, and identity shift, so too must our views about sex and sexuality.

Along with that, we also need a radical reinvention of love. Only when we have exposed the myths about sex and love at the core of our culture can we hope to find new ground on which to walk. In *The Radicality of Love*, philosopher Srécko Horvat explores the tension between twentieth-century revolutionaries and their resistance to and fear of love. He charts the sexual revolutions that attended various revolutionary movements in our recent history and the suppression of them that followed soon after. Revolution is love and love is revolution, Horvat argues. But all too often revolution is also about power and control, overthrowing one oppressive power in the name of revolution only for that revolution to fall into the same power traps. Love is about refusing particular kinds of power—power that dehumanizes, controls, and abuses. Revolution is also about energy—as is love and sex—and revolutionaries need to direct their energies into their causes, not into affairs of the body or heart. In this way, sex and love become dangerous to the success of a revolution, hence the ensuing repression.

In *The Radicality of Love*, Horvat also writes of the challenge when love and sex become habit and routine, and when our views become accepted without reflection. All of this precludes the true sexual revolution. Horvat concludes his book by using the Christian image of the trinity to outline a relationship between individuals and revolution. Love is nondirectional but relational between all three elements of the trinity. He claims, "God is revolution and love coexists between them all."

7

Thoughts on Death

Confront a corpse at least once. The absolute absence of life is the
most disturbing and challenging confrontation you will ever have.
—David Bowie

For many years, and in a number of different settings, I was a
pastor. In denominational, nondenominational, and completely
deconstructed, experimental community environments, I
preached and taught and prayed and did all the stuff associated
with church and religious communities. I met people at the
best and worst moments of their lives: births and marriages, the
beginnings and ends of life and love. If I were forced to choose, I
would prefer to preside at funerals rather than weddings. Funerals are where you get to be in solidarity and communion with
people at their most painful and lowest, yet there is often a sense
of hopeful humanity, marked by grief though it may be. But
funerals can bring us to places of honesty and openness seldom
found elsewhere. Shit gets real.

By the time I was seventeen, two of my friends had died. I
wore black for a year and dropped out of school during that
time. My friend Tim died by suicide not long after we had gone
to what was my first ever live concert: the Temptations at the
Royal Albert Hall in London. To this day, I cannot play their

music without thinking of Tim. I won't say much about his suicide; I have lived under the same shadow of depression for much of my life. It was shocking and sad and a fucking waste of his life, but I understood what he was going through (and I still do).

Simon Critchley says suicide is impossible. He derives his view from Freud and links it to the experience of melancholy. Suicide is impossible, he says, because the melancholic person experiences a division between who they are and an aspect of themselves that has been lost. He calls it the "hated other." The person who dies by suicide is ultimately not themselves but rather the hated other. This is not suicide, Critchley says, but murder—murder of the hated other that I am.

My friend Kevin died in a car crash on the way back from a club we had both been at together. I went home with someone else in a different car and was woken the next day with the news of his death. His parents visibly aged overnight, and his once outgoing and cheerful dad became a broken man for the rest of his life. Kevin's was the first body I ever saw laid out in a mortuary (another friend and I picked out his clothes for the casket). I can still conjure the smell, and I remember being taken aback by how cold he was when I touched his forehead. The mortician had done a terrible job on Kevin's hair, making him look like a banker, so we fixed that. It was obvious to me that some transition had taken place, that his flesh and blood had become something else. Whatever it was, I was certain he wasn't there anymore. I couldn't express it, and I hadn't any religious or philosophical ideas about mortality to draw upon then, but I knew it was brutal and complete. Kevin was gone.

Since then, I have spent a lot of time with people as they die, so I know something of the trajectory of a person's last days. Occasionally, I can predict their last breath to within a few hours. Like most everything else in life, it unfolds with a particularity—what Samuel Gross called "the rude unhinging of the machinery of life"—and it happens in such a predictable series that once you've experienced it a few times, it becomes very familiar.

Some people die well. Once, when I was working at a church in Los Angeles, I visited a man in the hospital whom I barely knew. His wife often helped with a homeless food program that the church hosted. She wasn't really a churchgoer; she just believed in trying to give something back to the community. But, regardless of her lack of interest in religious practice, her husband was dying, and she needed someone to speak with him. I think I was the least-likely looking minister available, which seemed to be what she wanted. He was in his late eighties, and his wife was there with him. She looked amazing, as she always did, stylishly cutting her own path through the sartorial landscape. The man was fantastic too. "I've had a good life," he said. "I've known wonderful people and had a long and happy marriage, and now it's time for me to go." He was a lifelong Episcopalian but wanted no prayer-book ending. He told me he didn't believe in an afterlife. He wanted nothing stodgy for his funeral, just lots of love and hopefully martinis for everyone after the service.

After he died, his ceremony was brilliant. All these old-school Hollywood people showed up. Not the plastic-surgery mob or the old Beverly Hills money crowd, but the arty types. It was as if they had all stepped out of a bohemian past. His wife was dressed to the nines and the attendees had been invited to wear anything but black. He was well eulogized, as one of the great Marvel comic creators was amongst his friends. Shaken by the loss but gamely rising to the occasion, the man delivered tales of his friend's life well-lived and of their friendship over decades. Copious martinis were served afterward, fueling a celebration of a person who would be missed but also remembered for his wit, grace, and kindness.

The worst funeral I ever conducted was for a little boy who died of a genetic disease that ate him up before he was even ten years old. The deeper tragedy was that in spite of the odds against it—the medical probability was almost zero—his younger brother had the same condition, which meant the family was facing a repetition of the same event in a couple years' time. My opening words at that funeral were, "This is fucked up." And it was. The family's grandmother was hostile to religion, a nonbeliever ironically angry at God, but she liked me because I swore at the funeral. To be honest, I didn't swear for dramatic effect. It's just all I had to say.

The hardest thing about that funeral was standing with the parents at the grave while the bulldozer covered his little coffin with dirt. Forget the idea of gravediggers carefully crafting a space in the earth. Graveyards are mechanized and industrialized, making it even harder to watch with the humanity removed just a little from the event. Digging a hole six feet into the earth must be incredibly difficult for the bulldozer operators, but they caused the whole earth to shake like an earthquake. This was fitting, because the whole thing felt like a psychic earthquake, a total shattering of the ground beneath this family's feet. Everything vibrated. The sight of that backhoe dragging mounds of earth toward the hole and the sound of it thudding onto the coffin—that's a sound I am in no hurry to hear again. There was silence when the bulldozer finished and the three of us stood there. It felt like eternity, but at least I was able to leave and go back to my life. The parents, on the other hand, were going to the hospital to tend to their other son. It was fucked up. Life is like that sometimes, and there is no explanation beyond that, especially one that includes God.

I find the defense of God at funerals to be the highest form of bullshit. To me there is nothing redeemable about God in such situations, and those who feel funerals are a good place to instruct people on God's bigger plan or some other spiritual platitude are missing the point completely. I get that they want to comfort people, but it usually comes across as an exercise in affirming their own beliefs in the face of a circumstance that challenges the base of our own views on God.

There is a verse in the Bible by the apostle Paul that declares, "O death, where is thy sting?" (1 Cor 15:55). It's a statement about the power of Christ's death and resurrection and how for Paul, this means that the "sting" of death is taken away. Understanding this gave Paul a profound sense of comfort and inner strength to continue to do the work he felt called to. I have never particularly liked this Scripture. I think I may not have experienced resurrection in the same visceral way that he seems to have. I applaud Paul's sentiment and recognize that he was trying to affirm something that might transform our understanding of death and mute its emotional impact, but I have felt death's sting so often that no amount of religious belief seems to eradicate it. It takes more than a statement of belief for someone to overcome the finality of human existence, and whatever Paul meant, I doubt he intended it to be invoked as some kind of remedy for grief and loss without the experience that brought him to say such a thing. We spend so much time trying to keep death away from us, but it's the one guarantee in life.

Some people try to mitigate death's impact because they believe death is not the end. Their religions offer an elaborate explanation of what comes after. Christianity, like most religions, has developed a scheme for handling death, with Christ's death being the ultimate finger raised to the power of death over us and our psyches. Declaring that death's power has been broken is a common trope for people familiar with Christianity.

Religion has done a good job of developing complex theories about the potential afterlife in order to help us find hope when we lose those we love. But death stings like a scorpion and, once bitten, you're never the same. I believe in the afterlife—the life that comes after us (this notion came from an interview between Critchley and my friend Kester Brewin when Kester was researching for a book he was writing)—but whether there is a future for me beyond my last breath is unknown and I have little opinion about that. There was life before me and there will be life after me—this is what I know. Immortality doesn't appeal to me. As Andy Warhol once said, "The worst thing that could happen to you after the end of your time would be to be embalmed and laid up in a pyramid. . . . I want my machinery to disappear."

I think other people's deaths can teach you about your own life and your own death. I could quote Martin Heidegger's theory of "being-toward-death": it is certain, it is indeterminate, it is not to be outstripped, and it is non-relational. His theory is that we gain a more authentic perspective about life as we grow when we have death as a sort of guiding or mentoring force. Or something like that! It's not an orientation but a way of being. It's a nice theory, but I resonate with the songwriter Jackson Browne more. Browne is one of the best death philosophers/theologians, if you ask me. In the song "For a Dancer," written for a friend who died in a fire, Browne expresses his inability to understand death. Like all of us, his friend, who was a dancer, has one dance they must do alone: the dance of death. Beyond that, Browne can only express ideas about death in the abstract and the poetic:

I don't know what happens when people die
Can't seem to grasp it as hard as I try
It's like a song playing right in my ears
That I can't sing
I can't help listening

Death is like a song you can't help listening to, but even though it's in all our ears, no one can sing it, because it's the one great mystery of life. This is the best I can do with death, and it's why I think any theory of an afterlife is precisely that: just a theory and a guessing game.

8

A Theology of Kissing

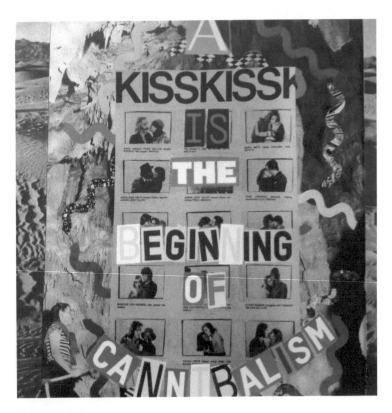

KISSKISS, Collage by me

"Love begins with a smile, grows with a kiss . . ."
—Augustine of Hippo

The kiss of friendship
   The kiss of charity
   The kiss of folly
   The illicit kiss
   The holy kiss
   The platonic kiss
   The lingering kiss
   The air kiss
   The kiss of peace
   The welcoming kiss
   The Judas kiss
   The kiss-off
   The French kiss
   The farewell kiss

The history of kissing is a fascinating aspect of our existence, but many people take the physical exchange of kissing for granted. The *Kama Sutra*, the ancient Sanskrit writings on sexual behaviors, devotes a whole chapter to various types of kisses, from the askew kiss to the farewell kiss. Some say the Greeks learned about kissing when Alexander the Great invaded India in 326 BCE, but Homer writes of kisses almost a thousand years earlier in the *Iliad* when he describes King Priam kissing the hand of Achilles in a plea for the return of his son's body.

But where kissing came from, nobody seems to know. Some believe it emerged from kiss-feeding in cultures where mothers feed their babies by passing masticated food from mouth to mouth. Regardless, this most intimate human action continues to fascinate us.

In his *Three Essays on the Theory of Sexuality*, Freud wrote that an individual's formative relationship to the world is an oral one, breastfeeding being what he called the "prototype of every relation of love." On child development, Freud noted how one will often suck their thumb or caress—but never kiss—themselves. He posited that children will kiss others on the mouth because they cannot kiss themselves there. Kissing is part of what he terms the polymorphous perversity of children. It's a perversion only in the psychoanalytic sense that it can be a substitute for genital intercourse. Kissing is integral to Freud's sexual development theory, which also describes the process of splitting that occurs when the need for nourishment and the need for pleasure diverge. Splitting happens when the child no longer needs the nutrition of the breast yet still desires its pleasure, thus birthing a new pleasure, what Freud calls sexual satisfaction. Kissing, as an element of sexual satisfaction, is a way out of the chaos of birth and into the development of one's life.

Humans can experience many intimacies, but apart from sex, perhaps nothing is more intimate than kissing. The touch of lips to lips, or even tongue to tongue—it is a mark of closeness and not something to be rushed into. The mouth is a portal into our bodies for those things we take in from the world that keep us alive: nutrition, water, air. But things also emerge out of the mouth: words, ideas, hopes, dreams. We announce ourselves to the world and to each other through our mouths with our shrieks, laughs, cries of joy and pain.

To kiss is also to exchange breath; you cannot kiss someone else without breathing into one another. I think there is a theological idea in that.

According to the Bible, humanity came alive with a kiss of sorts. God, it says in Genesis 2:7, breathed into the nostrils of Adam and he came alive. Kissing always involves an exchange of breath—that's what makes it so intimate, so primal. In addition to that initial kiss, the Bible is full of every kiss imaginable—kisses of covenant, welcome, even erotic kisses. "Let him kiss me with the kisses of his mouth," cries the lover in Song of Songs (1:2).

A kiss is a micro story, a world in and of itself. One of the most well-known micro stories is perhaps the kiss between Judas and Jesus on the night of Christ's betrayal. It has been captured by numerous artists throughout the ages. In Giotto's rather flat, pre-oil paint tableau, Judas's cloaked arm covers both men like a blanket and their lips barely touch. Caravaggio's depiction is of a passionate clash between the two men as armed soldiers press in around them. In this portrayal, Jesus's arms are stretched out before him like he is about to be handcuffed. A soldier is moving toward him as Judas grabs his shoulder, pulls him in, and presses his traitorous lips against Jesus's cheek. It's a hasty kiss, but it's filled with a world of things caught in that most intimate moment: betrayal; exposure; violation; collusion against love, not for it; and conspiracy with enemies of kindness and compassion. Those soft lips briefly pressed to flesh shifted the axis of humanity—at least, that's how the story goes.

It was also a kiss of identification. According to an eighth-century gnostic account, Jesus was a bit of a shapeshifter. He sometimes appeared as a young man and other times as an old one; he looked different every time. So, Judas needed to kiss the man whose identity was indefinable to mark him as the one to be arrested. An interesting notion, perhaps it can simply be seen as an attempt by the authors to capture the tragedy of such a moment marked by this act of tenderness.

A few years back, I wrote a song about this kiss from Judas's perspective. it was inspired by and adapted from a poem by Brendan Kennelly called *The Book of Judas*, a four-hundred-page epic poem.

My steps are slow
I cover ground
My thoughts are flying
All around
I lift my eyes
And see his face
My thoughts are flying
Every place

I'm not sure what I said
I'm not sure what I did
I reached out in tenderness
And planted a kiss

I kissed the tired legend in his eyes
I kissed the women standing by his side
I kissed the silence
Kissed the tears
I kissed his daring love
I kissed his daring, daring,
Daring love

I've long been fascinated by this moment, perhaps because I like kissing so much. Or perhaps it's because, while I can in no way claim the same kind of experience as Jesus, I *can* say I have been betrayed by a kiss more than once, and that I too have betrayed with a kiss. It is part of the pantheon of kisses with which I am intimately familiar.

Kissing is a funny thing. You likely did it without thought when you were young. Then it became almost repulsive—gross or yucky, as kids will say—until the moment it was not gross anymore. Then kissing someone became an almost blind obsession.

I remember the obsessive desire in my teens to kiss a particular girl. Let's be honest: in its initial phase, we desire to kiss anyone who will let us, but there is always someone in particular we dream of kissing. The idea of anything more, like sex, seems way too difficult to imagine then, but kissing means something. And that moment of success when we kiss someone for the first time? We learn something about ourselves that we didn't know before—we feel passion, the rush of desire, and hope and want and lust and love, all because our lips met another's.

I have had many memorable kisses. I've been lucky to have been kissed often and kissed well. Most of those kisses sink into the deep well of history, memorable at the time but not remembered later. That's not because they have no value; they just don't stand out. But I have had one kiss that was like no other. It wasn't the best kiss or the most passionate, but it was different from every other kiss in my life because it was named before it was given: the calculated kiss.

A few years ago, I met a woman at a conference in Arizona. We stayed in touch with each other after returning to our mutual homes, and found ourselves slowly moving toward a relationship and intimacy with each other. Still, there were mitigating factors between us, not the least of which was that we didn't live in the same town, not even the same state. This placed certain limits upon us, but thankfully FaceTime and phone calls facilitated our long conversations and growing interest and desire. Even so, it still placed our connection in an unfamiliar environment to both of us, given that neither of us had ever tried a long-distance relationship before.

We made decisions about the status of our relationship online, before we were ever both in the same room. We flirted and declared our interest in moving toward intimacy and in having a relationship with each other. Most of all, we shared our desire to kiss one another.

Eventually, she came to visit for the weekend, and we had to confront an elephant in the room. The kiss we had been speaking about for weeks—this kiss that would initiate a new phase in our relationship, shifting its axis from friendship to romance—was somehow imbued with an extraordinarily intimidating power. And we didn't kiss. It wasn't that we didn't want to or had changed our minds, but we had built up anticipation for this kiss and suddenly it meant more than the sum total of its parts.

There we were, two people looking to each other for something—not everything, but something—and the kiss was our boundary. We had both approached it and now we were stuck. We had discovered in each other things that offered us hope and warmth and care, but we couldn't find our way to a kiss.

Finally, we talked about it and she suggested something that changed everything. "We should have a calculated kiss," she said.

What is a calculated kiss? Well, by calling it calculated it is by default not spontaneous. It is intentional, planned, and purposeful. It has an end goal. For us, the goal was to bring all the things we had explored via long distance into the room with us. We were to make present all our hopes and desires expressed while we were apart. In doing so, we would bring together the disparate parts of us that were scattered all over by the dynamics of twenty-first-century digitally mediated romance, and perhaps even bring together the pieces of our hearts that were scattered by our own histories of love.

A boundary-breaking act, the kiss signaled our desire to overcome trepidation. So, for the first time in both our lives, we went in for a calculated kiss.

I still remember how we moved toward each other, eyes open at first but slowly closing. We held each other's hands for courage but we were surprisingly liberated by our decision to name the kiss. It wasn't just a kiss anymore; it was a calculated kiss. The kiss had become a gateway rather than an obstacle.

Our lips met, we laughed, then met our lips again, this time in commitment and passion. Banishing awkwardness, we breathed each other's breath and in turn breathed life and love into each other. Our calculated kiss became a tenuous, holy thread that knitted our two hearts together and opened up a world of love and romance.

We have had many kisses since, and they're better now because we've learned to read each other's bodies and emotions. But we've never forgotten the calculated kiss; it was the key to understanding what we have between us. It was the beginning of a conversation that silently expressed everything that was too deep for us to speak aloud. "A kiss," wrote Victor Hugo in *Les Miserables*, "and all was said."

PART II

Drugs: The Experiential

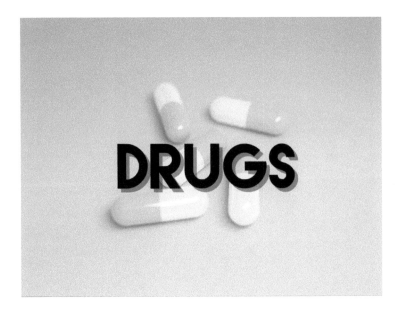

9

A Box I've Never Opened

I have a box I have never opened. It contains a gift from a friend who knew I did not want what was inside, but he bought it for me "just in case." The box contains a collarless clergy shirt with French cuffs and a couple linen clerical collars. It's from a place in London called J. Wippell & Co.

Let's be honest: it's just not for me. Dressing in clerical garb has always felt alien and I never could bring myself to embrace the collar. The clerical collar emerged in the first half of the nineteenth century, when clergy wanted to create a sense of separation between themselves and secular society. This idea—that to be a pastor is somehow to be other than the rest of the world—points to a problem that haunts the halls of institutional religion. I understand that many religious groups use distinctive dress as a means of self-identification and separation. But aren't there enough walls between the religious and the wider world? I'm not sure we need another one.

Of course, my lack of desire to wear a clerical collar goes deeper than that. Kierkegaard said that the most important thing for a person was to "grow in the soil" in which one feels most at home. Because of my own internal restlessness, feeling at home is quite elusive for me, particularly in religious environs. On the other hand, I feel quite at home in most places because I generally enjoy people (I get a little edgy around the overzealous, but I manage). I can appreciate what they are up to, but I often feel distant, so I largely keep to myself, stumbling around as if I'm searching for a black cat in a dark room.

Ultimately, I rejected the gift because the clothing didn't feel right. It wasn't home. It took seven or eight years for that gut instinct to turn into lived experience.

10

Play Fucking Loud

My therapist has told me many true things. The second truest thing he ever told me was that I have used self-destruction to deal with situations in which I felt stuck. But the very truest thing he ever told me was that I was a fucking idiot. This is why I go to him: I trust people who swear when the occasion calls for it.

I become self-destructive with some regularity, roughly every decade or so. I actually thought I'd given up on it for a while, but let's face it, we don't change much. We can become more aware of how we work and what makes us tick, but knowledge and action are two different things. I often resort to the lullaby of old spectral voices that have haunted me for much of my life, particularly whenever I feel helpless against the challenges ahead of me. I writhe, wrestle, and conspire against myself. It's not a good thing—it causes me pain and others heartache, it creates turmoil, and things can get ugly. But sometimes it feels as though it's the only way I can overcome myself and get to where I want to be.

Years ago, I desperately wanted out of a particular working situation but I didn't know how to do it. There were too many things pulling at me and I am prone to let things go for a long time, even when they make me unhappy. And I was very unhappy, caught up in an increasingly bureaucratic and corporate environment. God knows I have no time for any of that. I should have gotten out sooner, but I was living for a single hour a week when I could play music with friends, talk about life, and see a gathering of people become a community, a room filled with people I was actually interested in knowing better.

But the problem with living for a single hour a week is all the other hours one has to endure in order to get to there, and I had become an angry, frustrated, seething mess. It wasn't just about me; I'd already left a couple wounded souls in my wake, victims of my frustration and unhappiness, because I also withdraw from those who love me even when I'm not all right. And I had been so not all right. Someone I love had been telling me for ages that I needed to deal with what was making me unhappy, but I ignored that advice and continued reveling in my unhappiness until it all came to a head and I pulled that destructive trigger again. It became a veritable clusterfuck, traumatic and liberating at the same time. I was fired. It was humiliating, and I was ashamed, but it also got me out of a situation that I didn't feel I could get out of any other way. I figured that if I made it impossible for me to be there then I would have a way out. So that's what I did. Stupid, and I knew it at the time, but I did it anyway. I'm good at self-destruction, even though I don't wish to be. I think I felt I deserved the shame, and even liked the shame that came with those destructive tendencies.

I have since realized that while I was practicing self-destruction, I was betraying myself. There are two kinds of self-betrayal—I learned this from Bob Dylan. On July 25, 1965, Bob Dylan played his first ever electric concert at the Newport Folk Festival. In March of that year he had released *Bringing It All Back Home*, one side of which was electric. Just a few days before the concert, he released the single "Like a Rolling Stone," a rock song rather than folk. The response to Dylan going electric was seismic. Fans of traditional folk who regarded Dylan as a champion of their musical form were angry, while rock fans welcomed him with open arms. Dylan proceeded unbothered by either view and just made his music.

On tour in the UK in 1966, Dylan played a concert in Manchester, England. At the end of one song, an audience member infamously screamed at him: "Judas!" Dylan's response was revelatory. Turning to his band, he uttered three words: "Play fucking loud," and they launched into "Like a Rolling Stone."

The song is about change, about someone disillusioned with who they have become. The audience that night was divided because some of them wanted Dylan to be one thing and he turned out to be another. By going electric, he became a Judas to them. In breaking out of old formulas, he betrayed their cause. But this change also heralded something positive for Dylan. His betrayal made new things possible for him creatively: new musical sounds, new creative horizons, new permutations of his poetry. Naming him a Judas seemed only to inspire Dylan to become the person he wanted to be. It liberated him. His music since then has been a smorgasbord of styles and personalities; there is nowhere he won't go and nothing he won't try. He has lived an unparalleled creative life.

The lesson here—one I am still trying to learn—is that we betray ourselves when we allow external pressures to limit us. These betrayals cost us a richer, more authentic sense of ourselves and they steal our opportunity to live the lives we want to live. But there is another kind of self-betrayal, one in which we betray who we have been in order to become something, or someone, else.

Self-betrayal and self-destruction are born of the same frustration. Both might eventually get you where you want to be, but one empowers you while the other leaves you stuck. In both situations, we have to bear the pain and agony of those who want us to remain where or who we are. So, take a cue from Dylan: play fucking loud.

11

Migraines and Melancholy (Or Knowing One's Darkness)

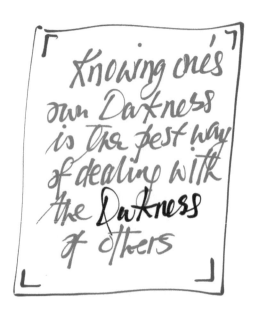

A riff on Jung's notion of the shadow self, iPad sketch by me

My life has been marked by a couple of Ms: migraines and melancholy. I have dark days when the seductive lure of nothingness intoxicates me. I don't share this because I am proud of it or because I want you to feel sorry for me. I say it because it is part of my life, my struggle for existence. Usually, I am drawn back from the edge by the pull of life, the possibility of something that can't be named. Whatever it is, it's certainly not optimism. I believe in life, I guess, and it continues to pull me back from the brink.

Melancholy is often linked to depression and sadness, but it has a character all its own. Freud said there was a difference between melancholy and its cousin, mourning, but they were both responses to loss. Mourning takes place in the conscious mind and deals with the loss of a specific thing—a loved one, for instance. Melancholy, however, occurs when a person deals with a loss they are unable to specify, so it takes place in the unconscious mind. Melancholy is this sense of loss, of what the sufferer does not know, but that loss colors and shapes the way they look at the world. It's an indescribable nothing, dressed up as an inexplicable something that cannot be named or understood. Freud believed mourning is healthy and melancholy is not. He said we need to learn to mourn, lest we fall prey to melancholia and die with all the nameless deaths it celebrates.

It also used to be said that melancholy affects those with too much time to think, so it came to be seen as a malady of the upper classes. The English are particularly known for their melancholia; it became known as the English disease in the sixteenth century, a time noted for its increased awareness of mental illness and suicide.

I don't seek out melancholy, nor do I revel in it. It comes upon me seemingly out of nowhere, but I own it and sit in it until it passes, which it generally does. Then the light comes back on in my life and I forget whatever it is that I have lost but cannot specify, that source of my melancholy.

I experience melancholy often, so take this with a grain of salt, but I don't think melancholy is always a negative thing. Or perhaps I have just learned to live with it while I try to name that unnamable thing deep inside me that might turn my melancholy into something valuable. In a society that obsessively champions positive mental attitudes and the pursuit of happiness, melancholic ache is often seen as a liability. But in my experience, a bit of melancholy will push you toward two things: beauty and wisdom. Not a shallow pristine beauty, but beauty forged from life and living—the beauty of life in all its ragged glory. Beauty that emerges in spite of the losses, pains, and struggles life brings us. The kind of beauty the romantics wrote of in their gothic novels, or the beauty of Lucian Freud's portraits—beauty that you can see when you acknowledge that life is tough and a struggle and at times almost unbearable, and yet you keep living. And the wisdom emerges when you realize that although there might be lots in life to feel disappointed about—injustice, violence, inequality—the answer is not to gloss these things over but rather to acknowledge them, to own the fact that life is unfair. Then we might be able to find ways to address these issues.

Long before he became a recording artist, Leonard Cohen wrote poems and novels. *Beautiful Losers*, published in 1966, is sometimes considered one of the first postmodern novels. It's a tale about a seventeenth-century Mohawk Indian saint caught in a love triangle. The book, which was not a great literary or commercial success, explores mysticism, sexuality, and other radical ideas spawned at the height of the era's youth counterculture. I have carried one line from the book around with me for some time: "How can I begin anything new with all of yesterday inside me?" That's what melancholy feels like—this overwhelming sense of the impossibility of a future because of what lurks inside. It's this viselike grip that a ghostly past holds over me.

The other M that marks my life is migraines.

The taste of cold metal in my mouth
The hiccups
The floaters in my eyes
The stiffness in my neck
The pain of sunlight
The strange cocoon my head is in
The wave of nausea
The flash of fire through my brain
The garbled words
The yawning
The gathering storm in my mind
The garbled words
The crippled thought process
The heaviness of limbs
The needling
The throbbing vein in my temple
The twitch in my eyes
The ineffectiveness of remedies
The desperate wish for a Coca-Cola
The lack of appetite
The desire for sleep
The insomnia
The restlessness
The swirls and eddies
The flashing light
The strange muffled hearing

I can't say much else about migraines. They come, like melancholy, from nowhere. The clue is that metal taste in my mouth, but by then it's already too late—once it sets in, I'm along for the long and painful ride. They last twenty-four to thirty-six hours on average and I try to function as best I can, but I feel horrible. And once it goes, I have a migraine hangover.

12

Creative Chaos

It has been virtually impossible to live on the west side of Los Angeles, as I have for the past few decades, and not have conversations about two things: Coachella and Burning Man. Burning Man, which began as a yearly ritual on Northern California's coast, has become a seminal countercultural event. Black Rock City, the site of the annual burn in the Nevada desert, draws thousands of people from all over the world for an experience like no other. Over a few days in late August, thousands gather and create a temporary city in the desert. Burning Man bills itself as a global movement and is built on ten principles that were created by its Man founder, Larry Harvey. They include things like radical inclusion, gifting (there is no money exchanged at Burning Man), self-expression, and communal effort. It culminates with the "burn," the central symbolic ritual, during which a giant wooden sculpture is set alight.

Burning Man has been described as many things: a temporary city, an alternative community, and a temporary autonomous zone (TAZ) event, driven by radical self-expression combined with a commitment to avoiding significance. In the book *After-Burn: Reflections on Burning Man*, writer and journalist Erik Davis called this the "insidious net of meaning." Davis now spends his time exploring alternative culture groups, such as Burning Man, that dot the twenty-first-century landscape. For him, the Burning Man experience is characterized by this avoidance of significance, the need to explain everything and give it a sense of deep meaning. This is what he means when he says that Burners (the term Burning Man attendees are known by) create an environment free from the net of meaning.

Almost everyone in LA has an opinion about Burning Man. Some dismiss it as a new-age bacchanal, while others hope the radical social and creative ideas that fuel it will take hold in the wider culture and "really change things."

The questions raised in many of the circles I move in are related to the dynamic between Burning Man and religion, and spirituality and the sacred/profane. At one time, the lines between the sacred and the profane seemed much clearer. The sacred encompassed the beliefs and practices that express our understanding of and are connected to our notions of the divine. It covered everything that exists beyond the everyday experiences of life. The sacred was also experienced and practiced in certain spaces, be they churches, temples, mosques, or other religious places. The profane was connected to the everyday experiences of life, what we could discover and understand through our senses. I once knew a woman who went every year and touted Burning Man's alternative spiritual dynamics, its rejection of dogma and doctrine, the ways it intertwined the intangible and material, and its profane and sexual means of connecting with the sacred. She typically attended while dressed only in blue latex, driven by a commitment to explore sexual and hallucinogenic experiences. I also know a few groups of Christians who go to evangelize or "be a presence for God," whatever that means. However, the unbridled sexuality, widespread drug use, and other wild and hedonistic goings-on at Burning Man have muddied the waters as to what exactly Burning Man is. Is it a spiritual experience? Counterculture nonsense? New age mumbo-jumbo? A demonstration of society's long and slow descent into moral depravity?

Burning Man might be all of those things at once, given that the gathering is about radical, individual self-expression but I also believe the drive undergirding Burning Man is the desire for some kind of sacred experience. What makes the event sacred is its profanity—or perhaps, the way in which the sacred and the profane intersect. In this it reflects much of the way in which religion in our time is sensate and empirical. Harvey writes, "Beyond belief, beyond the dogmas, creeds, and metaphysical ideas of religion, there is immediate experience." Perhaps this provides a clue to the essential dynamic of Burning Man's collective experience, and the dynamic that links it to broader and more mainline currents in spirituality.

Spirituality takes many forms, but in our time it is essentially built on personal experience. William James, who wrote *The Varieties of Religious Experience* in 1902, noted that experience, rather than belief, was at the root of religious life. James turned our attention away from the collective nature of religion, from its institutions, creeds, and dogmas, and put a spotlight on the subjectivity at the heart of religious experience. Burning Man's transformative experiences, wrapped up in a technicolor coat of hedonism, might seem a long way from traditional religious expression. Its attendees are techno-spiritualists and psychedelic experimenters, and eco-warriors and sexual explorers; there are vegans and cocktail camps; there are hippies and rainbow people, and people of every stripe and type, all doing their own thing. Burning Man doesn't present a singular experience. The myriad experiences people have at Burning Man *are* its spiritual component, and become the currency of its ritual form and its means of sustainability.

Like many forms of American spirituality, Burning Man is riddled with the apocalyptic. Now a well laid-out, temporary city, Burning Man is haunted by the conditions under which it operates: its apocalyptic notion is the consumerist, capitalist, military-industrial complex that rules the world outside its borders. Burning Man acknowledges, dismisses, and mocks that world through its gift economy, art, and hedonism, and throws itself wide open to the void that exists when those things are stripped away or rejected. But the void Burning Man celebrates is not nothing: it is a creative chaos.

Chaos is a reminder of impermanence, which lies at the heart of the event itself. Burning Man's time of excess and extravagance lasts a week, then it disappears without a trace, leaving the desert as empty as it was before, as though nothing ever happened. It's not that it's meaningless; it just has no meaning except what lies beneath the creativity and the chaos in the void between the apocalyptic and the utopian. This is the space opened up by Burning Man. It does not attempt to package or create a charter of necessary experiences. The idea is that we all must deal with the void in whatever way works for us. Burning Man is spirituality gone wild, perhaps the only form of spirituality that might survive in our times.

13

Dressing the Sacred

A few years ago I was approached by an editor at a publishing house to see if I was interested in writing a book on religion and U2. I had just taught a class on the band's musical and spiritual journey and had already done most of the research on the topic, so it seemed like a no-brainer.

As I wrote the introduction and chapter outlines, I began my exploration with a deconstruction of Bono's clothing. I wrote about his sunglasses, shoes, and everything in between. You can discover a lot about U2's worldview from Bono's way of dress. After I sent the preliminary materials to the editor, their feedback wasn't positive. They were looking for something more Jesus focused, and while they thought the clothing approach was interesting, it didn't fit with their vision for the book. I understood to some degree. Fashion and religion are seldom discussed together. It is easy to overlook the importance of dress, particularly from a religious or theological perspective, given its tendency to favor the internal dynamics of the human condition.

"Clothes make the man," Mark Twain once said. Given that he owned twenty-two custom-made white cashmere suits, he may have been on to something. I have been interested in fashion and clothing for most of my life, ever since my first after-school job in a clothing store. Today, I am still fascinated with beautiful fabrics or the particular cut of a jacket. But I am more interested in how what we wear gives us a sense of ourselves.

The Italian philosopher Mario Perniola, in a 1989 essay called "Between Clothing and Nudity," argues that clothing is what gives humans a sense of being, that what we wear and how we wear it shapes our identity. When the subject of fashion comes up, many people's immediate responses are connected to Jesus's statement that we should give no thought to what we eat, drink, or wear. But these are things most of us think about often and carefully. Just walk into a coffee shop and listen to the particular permutations of drinks people order, or consider the growing foodie movement from veganism to food trucks, and you get a sense of the degree to which the simple acts of eating and drinking are filled with careful thought and reflection. So when it comes to clothing, there can be little argument that what we wear is, for most people, a very serious consideration.

We dress to impress, to hide and conceal. We use clothing for effect, decoration, self-expression, and sexual attraction. We use dress to express our gender and to show our religious affiliation, profession, favorite sports team. The list goes on. Long before we speak, our dress communicates messages that we all translate, judge, and respond to. We read one another's clothing and determine things such as age and socioeconomic status, but we also gauge moods, personality, and interests from it. I use the word *judge* intentionally, because we do make judgments based on what we encounter people wearing.

Some days, I dress up not necessarily to impress anyone, but because it makes me feel better about myself. When I am having a rough time, I turn toward more formal clothes. I spend time choosing what to wear, and I wear pieces that mean something to me and that I enjoy wearing (I also go to therapy, but that's for another essay). Something about the process boosts my confidence and gives me an emotional lift. People go shopping for the same reason. It's more than a distraction or a sign of our capitulation to materialism; the way we clothe ourselves goes deeper than the external elements.

While all of this reflects the personal decisions and emotions behind our clothing choices, clothing is never simply a personal matter. What we wear has an effect on others; it can shape lines of communication between us. The way we dress sends cues ranging from "Notice me!" to "Ignore me!"

If I were to say something about the challenge facing Christianity today, I would characterize it as a problem of appearance. For many, Christianity is dressed in a style long gone from this world. Practicing Christianity is like journeying into another time, glimpsing into history. Many people in religious circles critique our contemporary culture's preference for surface over depth, and they are concerned about the spiritual cost of a fascination with the superficial external at the expense of the internal.

The real issue is that many in the religious world are unable to dress themselves to fit the times—to dress their ways of speaking about God in such a manner that they can be interpreted and understood on their own terms in this world. I'm not simply talking about following fashion trends or attempting to be relevant (one of those bywords whose invocation means you are hopelessly out of touch).

A fashion blog I frequent, called *Threadbared*, featured an interview with theologian Cornel West last year. The interview's focus was not race, justice, or religion, but his clothing. West wears a daily uniform: a three-piece black suit (he owns five), a white shirt with cufflinks, and a scarf, tie, socks, and shoes—all black. In the interview, he linked his choice of clothing (like Johnny Cash) to his calling to bear witness to love and justice in a dark world. The clothes are an "extension of the man," West said. Fashion and dress offer us visual clues by which to approach our time, ways to read and interpret messages about our lives and the present cultural moment. A theology of fashion is one that reads the signs of the times and dresses accordingly, shifting not with the whims of seasonal trends, but with a sense of calling and intention.

I have been interested in a theology of fashion for quite some time. I came of age after the upheaval of the 1960s, when long hair on men was a focus of government debate in the House of Commons. But I was also around when similar public debates over punks and their degenerate dress and behavior filled the British cultural and political arteries. I realize that, for many, there are far weightier matters to address, but I am not the only one interested. When discussing what he termed the "lordless powers" in his Church Dogmatics lectures, theologian Karl Barth included fashion in his list of things like transportation and technology that operate as "demonic powers" in culture. "Who inspires and directs these processes, which are not a matter of indifference to the feeling for life and all that it implies?" Barth asks. He was questioning where the authority and guidance for the way we shape our lives comes from. His response was that rather than coming from God, he believed some "released spirit of the earth" was responsible for the fashion industry's ability to generate such "horror and amusement" each season.

Now, there are questions about the fashion industry that can and need to be addressed—the role of advertising, marketing, and lifestyle branding, for instance—but these are secondary issues for me. I am more interested in the way dress functions as a visible code by which we communicate. The story of Adam and Eve is often both the beginning and end of most theological conversations about clothing, and it centers on the consequences of sin. But this is too shallow a read. The shame they felt for eating the fruit of the tree might not have been simply guilt for disobeying God, but a consequence of realizing they couldn't administer the wisdom and rule that came with the knowledge they had gained. In a sense, they weren't dressed for the job. I

said previously that the concept of nudity in our culture is insep-
arable from its theological signature.

The opposite is also true: how we dress is theologically linked
to this story too. This is not the Bible's sole story about the per-
tinence of clothing. It has many stories where the interplay of
dress and wisdom interconnect—Joseph's coat of many colors,
David cutting a corner of Saul's robe, Elijah's cloak, God's com-
mand to place tassels on the edge of priestly garments, John the
Baptist's camelhair clothing, the dividing of Jesus's cloak. The
color of your shirt runs deeper than dyes or threads—it's forever
entwined with something far more sacred than meets the eye.

14

Dirt

Years ago, a friend told me he thought the biggest problem with Christians is that they are afraid of dirt. He said the desire for purity puts a premium on postures that distance them from anything contaminating: the grime and messiness of life. "We send our broken away to get fixed," he said, "afraid that we will be tainted by their dirt, rather than standing alongside each other no matter what. But that's what you get when the institution is more important than its people or purposes."

Since then, I have come to recognize how right he was. In my experience, churches are sometimes not the best places to bring one's dirt; in fact, quite the contrary. All too often, our concern with purity means that those who gather dirt will find themselves ostracized. A community of people gathered in solidarity with their brokenness can quickly become a community where getting fixed is the order of the day and being clean is the goal.

But Christianity is a religion of dirt. Jesus walked in the dirt of the world, wrote in its dust, and gathered those around him who seemed the most sullied by life—tax collectors, prostitutes, and sinners of all shapes and sizes. When it comes to Christianity, if you lose the vulgarity, then you lose the religion. Like many other things, Christianity suffers from our tendency to domesticate, clean things up, and make them appealing to wider audiences. But it's a profane faith. After all, according to Saint Paul in one of his letters to the Corinthians, we are called to be the trash, the shit of the earth, and that is nothing if not base and vulgar.

One story in particular in the Gospel of Matthew makes me think about vulgar Christianity. After Jesus had called the tax collector Matthew to join him, he had dinner with a bunch of tax collectors and other assorted undesirables, much to the disdain of the present religious leaders. When they questioned Jesus's choice of dining partners, his response is one I have been thinking about for years: "Those who are well have no need of a physician, but those who are sick. Go and learn what this means: 'I desire mercy, not sacrifice.' For I have come to call not the righteous but the sinners" (Matt 9:12–13).

What strikes me about this encounter is the tension Jesus places between mercy and sacrifice. These two values pull us in different directions, and Jesus valued mercy above the other. What is the dividing line? To me it seems somehow connected to the company we keep. To his detractors, Jesus's dining partners represented the vulgar, the dirty, the unsavory. Their religion precluded associating with anything unclean. Theirs was a religion of limits and boundaries, exclusions and removals. But Jesus saw things differently. For him, crossing boundaries and associating with transgressors was the very heart of who he was, how he saw the world, and what he thought the gospel was all about. Whereas the Pharisees were afraid of sullying their religious perspectives, Jesus refused to sacrifice people in order to become clean.

Miroslav Volf, in his 1996 book *Exclusion and Embrace*, speaks of the "will to purity" that sometimes dominates the faith experience. In those situations, two dynamics manifest. First, people who threaten our pure and clean place before God are pushed away and become stigmatized. This is prevalent in the Bible regarding tax collectors, prostitutes, and other sinners, and Jesus resisted this potently. Second, religion increasingly takes on a vertical direction, and God becomes a singular focus at the expense of our fellow human beings. "Love the Lord your God and your neighbor" (Matt 22:37–39) is how Jesus interpreted the law, with both God and neighbors carrying equal value. But a religion obsessed with purity has a tendency to neglect human need.

Now, I don't think our hunger for sacrifice or purity is all wrong. Elsewhere, the Bible invites us to consider acceptable kinds of sacrifice. The problem is that something dangerous seems to happen whenever people do become obsessed with purity. Others get hurt and lives get damaged. How do we to navigate this? According to the radical theologian Thomas J. J. Altizer, we must seek the sacred not by saying no to the radical profanity of our time, but by saying yes to it.

In other words, we should not fear all the dirt around us. If we spend some time in it, we just might find our way to a different and more authentic religious experience.

15

Skulls

Selfie with skull

I have a skull fetish. Almost everyone does these days, it seems. I claim nothing special or exclusive about my relationship to skulls, except that I was an early adopter. And I'm not interested in them just for the aesthetics. Any old skull won't do. Lots of people who know me give me skulls, but most of them I don't like. That pirate or Halloween stuff, for instance, is not where my interest lies.

My fascination with skulls stretches back to my childhood, when I had an anatomy book that fascinated me, particularly the bones. Using the macabre pages of that book as source material for my own drawings, I developed a lifelong interest in bones and skeletons, death and dying.

There was one other inspiration for my preoccupation. The town where I grew up was home to a tiny one-room museum dedicated to Oliver Cromwell, leader of the Puritan army and the Lord Protector of England. It was nothing fancy—old, dusty documents, mostly—but it held a few items of interest: a Roundhead helmet, Cavalier uniforms, and other bits and pieces from the English Civil War era. It also had Cromwell's death mask.

Biology at school played a part alongside my art, and somewhere in the deep recesses of my youth I started collecting skulls—pictures first, then the real thing (or versions of it). They are trendy now, but my interest has always been more focused on the old idea of memento mori, or reminders of death. I like being reminded of mortality.

Skulls are classified as vanitas objects. Medieval artists often used things such as skulls, hourglasses, and old books to invite sober reflection on one's existence and to remind us that life is short and uncertain. Every skull has its own unique particularities, but they share a commonality in that everyone has one. Thus, skulls represent a side of life on which we seldom reflect: the unseen, the uncertain, and finitude.

I wonder if, on an unconscious level, we still employ skulls today to achieve that same ancient end. They serve as reminders of a deeper reality in the midst of the sea of empty cultural promises of happiness and unlimited possibility in which we precariously swim. Skulls remind us of life's limits and uncertainties.

Perhaps that's also why the Day of the Dead, Halloween, and

zombies and vampires are such pervasive images within our current popular culture. We don't speak about this knowledge we hold deep within ourselves, so instead we set the symbols in motion. Art critic Hal Foster calls this traumatic realism, a term he uses particularly in his writing about Andy Warhol's work. In traumatic realism, the artist takes on the nature of what shocks him as a mimetic defense against the shock. Perhaps that how skulls function for us, employed almost as a palliative (to reference Freud) that shields us, while simultaneously reminding us of the reality it represents.

We live with constant tension when we have very little cultural vocabulary to help us come to terms with reality. Skulls beckon us toward that reality, even as they remind us of what we are repelled by, or simply afraid of: death. All is vanity, the skull says.

16

Capitalism on Drugs (Or Our Love Affair with Non-Permanent Pharmacological Lobotomies)

Religion, Karl Marx famously declared, is the opium of the people. This sentiment generally dismisses religion as little more than an illegal drug. Marx believed one purpose of religion was to dull the senses and create fantasies for the poor, offering them a fulfilling afterlife in lieu of the happiness they couldn't afford in this earthly one. He also believed people in the midst of life's hardships need solace, which religion often provided.

We often misread Marx's quote because we view drugs, and opiates in particular, much differently today. In Marx's time, the opium trade was a massive economic boom for Britain. Opium was cheap and accessible, one of the few drugs available to the poor. It treated all kinds of ailments such as coughs, rheumatism, and menstrual complications. It was even given to children to help them sleep. Laudanum, a mixture of alcohol and opium, was called the aspirin of the nineteenth century and was readily available alongside cocaine and arsenic. Believed to also inspire creativity, opium was used as a hallucinogenic by writers such as Charles Dickens, Percy Shelley, and Samuel Taylor Coleridge. Laws eventually regulated opium use, but until viable alternative painkillers were introduced toward the end of the nineteenth century, virtually every area of society used opium in some fashion.

Anti-opium movements, fueled by new religious zeal, emerged at the end of the Victorian era. Organizations such as the Christian Union for the Severance of the British Empire with the Opium Traffic in 1888, sensational journalism, and the creation of evil characters in cheap novels such as Sax Rohmer's Dr. Fu Manchu series increased vilification of the East and opium in particular. By 1910, Britain had dismantled the India-China opium trade, and the drug was soon outlawed for its addictive tendencies. Opium soon melted into the netherworld of transgressive culture, making one generation's medicine the next's illicit escape hatch from reality.

A lot is happening in the pharmaceutical world today, both in mainstream and alternative spheres. While Big Pharma companies launch a continual stream of new drugs into circulation, experiments with psychedelics—particularly LSD and psilocybin (magic mushrooms)—are emerging in ways we haven't seen since the 1960s. The current exploration into psychedelics falls into two research categories: their medicinal or therapeutic benefits, or their ensuing drug-induced mystical experiences. Psychedelic experiences are believed by a number of researchers to be quite similar to what might be broadly called mystical experiences.

The current renaissance of interest in psychedelics began with a 2006 report by R. R. Griffiths et al. Focusing on people who had religious or spiritual associations but no experience with psychedelics, the report noted several benefits of psychedelics. For example, the stronger the mystical experience one encountered with psychedelics, the more they reported feeling freed from depression and other issues, including the fear of death. Their experiences were measured according to Hood's Mysticism Scale, developed in the 1970s by psychology professor Ralph Hood.

And the knowledge base keeps expanding. Peter Sjöstedt-H, an Anglo-Swedish philosopher, recently shared with me his studies on the role of psychedelics in philosophy. His interests lie in the more existential dynamics of mind-altering substances. In his 2015 book *Noumenautics*, he recounts his personal experiments with psilocybin, and its transformative effect on his life and views about consciousness, the nature of the self, and other philosophical notions.

Michael Pollan's 2018 *New York Times* bestseller *How to Change Your Mind* explores the history and resurgence of psychedelics, as well as his own experiences with them. Pollan describes how his experiences changed how he sees himself and the world, by challenging his largely material perspective of life and giving him a new perspective on his ego that liberated him from old mental ruts and habits. He offers therapeutic inspiration for others struggling with addiction, anxiety, or depression.

The history of altered consciousness and religious experiences is long and storied. Peyote, ayahuasca, and psilocybins have all been cited as integral to certain religious rites and practices around the globe. But still Christianity remains resistant to drug use. Most Christians I know are far more interested in microbrewed beer and gin. I attended a conference on faith and culture in the late 1990s at which one speaker passionately discussed the benefits of ecstasy in creating community. His talk sadly didn't leave much of an impact. Of course, the illegality of many of these substances can't be ignored. But it does seem that our culture is entering a new phase of its relationship with psychedelics.

The ugly truth is that we are a culture of pill-takers, and artist

Damien Hirst explores this in his work. His famous medicine cabinet installations and his photo-realistic pill paintings portray what he feels is our almost spiritual relationship to pharmaceuticals and our belief in the ability of drugs to provide for us what life cannot. From portrayals of drug packaging to shelves of neatly painted single pills in *The Tears of Jesus*, Hirst depicts medicines in ways that look perfect and pure at first glance. Upon closer inspection, however, each comes with mile-long lists of potential side effects. He challenges the promotion of these drugs as a panacea, highlighting our dependency on pills to fix what ails us. These drugs—such as oxycodone and fentanyl, linked to the current opioid crisis—enrich pharmaceutical companies while ensnaring countless people in webs of legalized addiction to pills that don't always deliver on their promises.

In his 2018 book *Narcocapitalism*, Laurent de Sutter explores what he calls the age of anesthesia. De Sutter connects our relationship with drugs from the anesthetics invented in the nineteenth century to things such as Prozac in the twentieth century. Arguing that we now manage large parts of our emotional lives with drugs, he looks at how the chemical outsourcing of our emotions developed alongside modern society. Our excitement, according to de Sutter, has become drug-induced, yet in spite of all the pills available to us we fail to understand why we remain depressed and tired. One possible explanation, he suggests, lies in the challenges facing surgeons before anesthesia. The surgeons needed to manage not only pain, but also the thrashing their patients exhibited in response to it, threatening their own safety and the surgeons' success. Anesthesia made it possible for the human body to be safely repaired, but the ensuing transformation of the body into inhuman matter meant the surgeons could forget that their patients had souls. De Sutter argues that narcocapitalism has stolen the soul of society, which is why we remain dissatisfied with medicine despite the promise of pills.

Psychedelics research might be one way that society is on the path to recovering its soul. Psychedelics' potentially transformational and mystical experiences indeed challenge how we think about the world. I don't think mystical experiences are necessarily religious or should lead to some kind of belief in a god or gods, but they remind us that there is a world beyond what we claim to know. Philosopher Eugene Thacker calls this the occulted world. Becoming aware of the occulted world is to become aware of things beyond our awareness, reminders that the world is bigger than our capacity to know.

The difference between Big Pharma and psychedelics is that pharmaceuticals address our various ailments but, much like the parallel wellness industry, seldom address the circumstances that might be causing all our anxiety, stress, and depression. There is little doubt in my mind that if studies continue to discover the benefits of psychedelics, then corporate medical culture will bandwagon these substances into the medicinal culture that serves capitalism.

This is why the counterculture's embrace of hallucinogens should not be dismissed. The spiritual side of these experiences—which isn't as scientifically provable, in spite of things such as Hood's scale—represents the transgressive shadow side of culture. Early embrace of psychedelic potential was taken to the streets in the counterculture of the 1960s. It was liberated from the confines of institutions and threaded through the decentralized web of the counterculture. It wasn't all good; it was wild and ungoverned. But magic mushrooms, like some spiritual experiences, grow best in the shadows of the wilderness.

17

My Own Judas

"I am my own Judas." So declares Oscar Wilde in a scene from the beautiful but tragic 2018 film *The Happy Prince*. The film—directed, starring, and written by Rupert Everett—follows Wilde into his exile after serving two years of hard labor in England's Reading Gaol prison for "gross indecency." *The Happy Prince* is wrapped around Wilde's story of the same name, which only adds to the pathos before our eyes.

This is not a film to see if you aren't in a good headspace, but it is one that should be seen. More than an acting triumph for Rupert Everett, the film is a glimpse into the abyss of another person's brokenness. In this age of blockbuster action movies and remake after remake of movies that weren't even great the first time around, it's good to sit in the dark of a movie theater and come face-to-face with ourselves and each other in our humanity.

In *The Happy Prince*, we meet Wilde as a shell of a man, still desperate for fame and acknowledgment, yet still prone to the same potentially destructive actions that got him into trouble in the first place. Everett's Wilde is a broken man, ostracized by friends and from society, making his way to France to find respite from the vitriol and the scrutiny.

It's a sad tale, interrupted by moments of desperation as Wilde attempts to make his exile work. But the man, at least in the film, is his own worst enemy—hence his Judas declaration. His love for Bosie, the son of the Marquess of Queensberry, destroys his life. After reigniting their relationship, Wilde is soon cut off from a small income from his wife's family, and he finds himself penniless and alone, a long way from the dizzy heights of his pre-prison fame. Flashbacks reflect on his former life and family, but the majority of this film lives inside Wilde's head as he falls deeper and deeper into decline.

Wilde's self-destruction was very grand and public. His post-prison life reveals that in spite of the awareness of his own folly that he gained while in prison, he is still capable of repeating his old patterns. This is no hagiography; this is Wilde at his lowest. But we are also made aware of the terrible and unnecessary brutality of his punishment. Wilde's crime was publicly displaying his homosexual relationships, particularly with the son of an aristocrat. The film notes at the end that seventy-five thousand men were posthumously pardoned in 2017 for their felonies—all those lives ruined for the crime of homosexuality. Tragic, indeed.

As Wilde lays dying, his two companions send for a priest to administer last rites and offer extreme unction. The priest asks Wilde when it was that he lost his way and departed from Christ. Barely conscious, Wilde opens his eyes and says, "Clapham Junction." Clapham Junction was the railway station where Wilde, after being sentenced for his crimes, was forced to sit in public—head shaven, shackled to a guard, and clothed in prison garb—and wait to be transferred to prison. As people in the area grew aware that Wilde was the prisoner on the platform, a hostile crowd gathered around him. For thirty minutes, he had no option but to sit through ridicule and verbal abuse while being spat upon by the public. This was where Wilde lost his way, and it came at the hands of people who added to his punishment by heaping scorn and abuse upon him. His declaration was an indictment of humanity, a telling reminder that we can so easily be emissaries for evil and not for good.

Wilde arrived to Clapham Junction already humiliated and was preparing to embark on a prison sentence that would destroy him physically and emotionally. Everett's performance captures the essence of how man's inhumanity can immensely damage a person's life. We forget so easily that we all are broken, that we all can perform acts of folly, that we all can be our own Judas.

18

Tattoos

I have six tattoos. They all have meaning and stories behind them, and they all represent particular moments in my life that demanded an inscription in my flesh. For example, a friend once texted me words of comfort and support in a difficult time, ending with the phrase "Survive and advance," and I now carry those words on my arm. My most recent one is a palm tree in honor of my thirty-year sojourn in Los Angeles, and a Nick Cave lyric I got with a friend to cement a relationship and a love.

By now, tattoos have claimed a place in contemporary society, and they no longer carry the taboo they once did. I think the trend is driven by the impermanence of our lives, the worlds we live in where things are always evolving and the body is the only constant we have to hold on to.

Once I was walking down a Soho street in London when I spied a man out of the corner of my eye whom I instantly recognized. It was the artist Lawrence Weiner. I love his work so much that I had once taken the typeface he uses in all his text art to form part of a work on my arm. That day on the street, I decided to do what I seldom do and approached him. He was sitting outside his hotel having a smoke and enjoying a moment of quiet. As we chatted, he was friendly and charming, and I told him about my love for his work. Then I thanked him for his work and his time, and I left.

The tattoo that Weiner's typeface appears in is of a skull with two small crosses and the phrase "Doubts and loves" in purple ink. The skull is from a photo I took of a skateboard deck made by Damien Hirst, another one of my favorite artists. The words come from a poem by Yehuda Amichai that begins, "From the place where we are right, flowers will never grow." The counter to this desire to be right that hardens our soils, Amichai writes, is that "Doubts and loves dig up the world." That phrase appeals to me because doubts and loves are both means by which newness comes to our lives. I decided to get it all in violet because I once met an Indian guru who told me it was a good color for me, without knowing it is one of my favorites. And I got the type done in Franklin Gothic Compressed, which Lawrence Weiner calls the "last of the working-class typefaces" because it essentially disappeared after the Helvetica font was created. I felt it was a good reminder of my own working-class roots. All of that meaning is wrapped into a couple inches on the surface of my skin. But surface is depth in the modern world.

Much of the religious world has a complex relationship with tattoos. Judaism forbids idolatry and consequently prohibits tattooing (Lev 19:28) and Christianity followed suit by outlawing tattoos at the Second Council of Nicea. In his letter to the Galatians, Saint Paul says, "In future let no man make trouble for me, for I bear the marks of Jesus branded on my body" (Gal 6:17). Those words are often interpreted symbolically, but thereafter many pilgrims began marking their bodies after visiting shrines or making sacred journeys.

Tattoos turn the body into a symbol. But for what? Sometimes tattoos are so personal that only the vaguest interpretation can be made without a conversation. Nonetheless, in this age when tattoos have broken out of their backstreet associations and designs have become more personalized, there is little doubt that they represent a semiotic response to life in the modern world.

In 2018, the rapper Post Malone attracted attention by revealing a new facial tattoo on Instagram. The words "Always Tired" appeared in fresh script under his obviously tired and bag-laden eyes. His followers' response was immediate, acknowledging that they too were also always tired. *Rooster* magazine, in a weekly roundup of music news, noted that with the tattoo, the artist was "representing the voice of an entire generation." Why is a young, successful, popular artist so tired—tired enough to permanently mark his face? And why does his tattoo resonate deeply with so many people?

In HuffPost, journalist India Benjamin offered an interesting perspective on the tattoo and the cultural conflict it raised. Many people believe millennials are tired because they are entitled and consequently miserable from failing to get what they want, so instead they stay up all night drinking and doing drugs. The real reason, she proffered, is a much longer list of grievances, from despondency about life linked to expectations without opportunity, as well as a growing disillusionment with media, politics, economics, and most things they have inherited from previous generations. Much of Benjamin's commentary focuses on millennial exhaustion, but I think it extends beyond the generational divides we often use to characterize the way things are.

Everyone I know is tired, exhausted, and burned out. It's one of the marks of our time. In 2000, in *Illness and Culture in the Postmodern Age*, David Morris created a biocultural story of illness. He wrote that illness differs with time and context; we don't become ill in the same way our parents and grandparents did, and we experience illnesses and cures that would have been unheard of to them. Always being tired might not often constitute an illness by itself, but I do think the cultural settings we find ourselves in—particularly the increased precariousness and uncertainty of life—contribute to the way we feel every day. Things hover beneath the surface of our daily existence like low-grade fevers waiting to break out. The gig economy; the vulnerability of relationships; political unrest; the turmoil over race, gender, identity, and refugees—all of that is piped to us in a continual stream of endless fearmongering. Then the addictive nature of social media traps us in a web of comparisons, celebrity, affluence, and perfectionism, driving us to think less of ourselves unless we compete with these perfect worlds presented via social media.

Part of the cause of all this exhaustion is our obsessive thinking about our own status in society and our envy of our peers who splatter their best lives over the web. The gift of technology is access and connectivity, but it curses us to feel that our lives need to keep pace with those of who we look up to. The hustle of technology and consumer capitalism has many dark sides, one of which is an environment of hyper-comparison that few of us are incapable of avoiding.

This is why I am troubled by the self-help industry. It gives people remedies to deal with the strains of life, but seldom takes the time to address the world people are so stressed by. We destress to deal with a life that creates stress. Is the "best life" sold to us online really the best option?

There's always another option: get some rest.

Doubts and loves, one of my tattoos

19

Love Is a Losing Game

I have spent much of my adult life wrestling with the complexities of religion, its effect on my own life and the world around me. So, when someone asked last night at dinner what my core spiritual value was, I felt a little stuck. I don't live my life by the rules of any key statements, and my core beliefs, if they do exist, aren't exclusively religious. That might be surprising given that my life has been so intimately wrapped up in religion.

"There is no God and we are his disciples," was my initial reply. Paraphrasing the philosopher John Caputo, when it comes to God I think in terms of insistence, rather than existence. I don't believe in a supernatural being who watches and controls everything, but I do think an insistence to live in particular ways is wrapped into the folds of our religiosity. So, I said that living a life of love is key for me and that such a life will do you no harm. But it *will* cost you.

Attempting to live a life marked by graciousness and loving kindness will fuck you up; it will expose flaws deep in your psyche; it will challenge your sanity daily; it will expose hypocrisies, weaknesses, and blatant bullshit like nothing else. And there will often be little in the way of positive result because, as Amy Winehouse once sang, "Love is a losing game." She was singing about romantic love, but I don't think it's very different with any other kind of love.

What I probably should have said is that I am just trying to be a nicer person, because that's the truth. There are so many assholes in the world, and I don't want to be one if I can help it. I have let go of so many lofty religious aims and drives, not out of resignation but because I don't think they work in people's lives. I came of age with forms of Christianity riddled with obligations to "win the world for Jesus" or "take back the culture." That kind of moralism made life more of a duty than a joy. I saw many people crumple under the weight of lives they were not capable of living once their resolve or willpower ran out. And I ran out of steam as well. I didn't walk away, but I did seek to reframe my thinking about these things.

Years ago, I saw U2 in concert. The band was touring on the back of its album *All That You Can't Leave Behind*. The tour's logo was the outline of a suitcase with a heart in the middle. I've always been interested in that album's title. It's a strange inverted statement—rather than thinking about what you take with you, what can you not afford to leave behind? It begs a different kind of inventory. Having traveled a lot in life, I know you can't take everything with you (I'm not a multiple-suitcase traveler), but some things you do: passport, socks, underwear. The basics.

When it comes to religion, I feel similarly. In its static form, we accumulate lots of stuff: ideas, dogmas, opinions, and doctrines on anything and everything. But when religion goes mobile, when it shifts and turns, when conventional wisdom is questioned and it's time to move on, a cull is called for. That heart in a suitcase became a talisman for me, giving visual shape to the one thing I can't leave behind: love. Some have told me it is not enough—that there is more to life, religion, and Christianity than love. But I don't think the problem is that love is not enough; it is that we are not ready for all that love entails.

20

The Sound of Failure

I have just finished teaching a two-week intensive class on theology and popular music. These classes are demanding, but they also yield fruitful conversations, as the immersion deep into a topic has a different dynamic than a class that stretches out over a regular term. In this class, I was attempting to synthesize meanings in popular music with the intersections, departures, and challenges of theological responses to the world around us. We covered the developmental history of pop music; some of its key genres, artists, and producers; the commerce of the music industry; and the role of technology and culture. It was too much stuff for two weeks, but we did our best to touch on at least some of this meaningfully.

On the final day, I sketched out a beginning posture to initiate a conversation between theology and popular music. Posture is the operative word because, for me, any act of theology first springs from a posture or attitude. This is, first and foremost, listening. If you don't listen, you can't hear. And if you can't hear, you can't fully understand. All too often, people approach theology with a preformed schema that they impose on any subject. Then what fits into the schema is accepted and the bits around the edges are cut off, dismissed, or negated. My approach—and what I hoped to pass on to my students—is that the bits that don't fit into our schemas might be the most helpful to us.

One of our key discussions in the class was the role mistakes and failures play in the development of popular music. Take Bill Haley and His Comets's song "Rock around the Clock." The song, which arguably launched rock 'n' roll into the mainstream, was recorded in forty minutes. It was so rushed that sounds levels weren't properly set, giving it a live sound that made it feel more rebellious and anarchic than it might have been in a more managed setting. The band recorded only two takes, which were spliced together to create the song. The whipcrack snare drum at the start of the song was a mistake they didn't edit out, and it became the signature sound of rock 'n' roll.

Or take the Police's song "Roxanne." Its opening features an atonal piano clang and a menacing cackle—that was the sound of singer Sting falling onto a piano. Sometimes unplanned moments bring the most creative and transformative elements to art—and to life.

Popular music is innately tied to technology. Record players, cassette machines, electric guitars, amplifiers, synthesizers—there is no pop music without technology, and it is often characterized by the limits of those technologies. Guitar distortion is the sound of something too loud for the medium that is supposed to carry it, but where would rock be without it?

The voice in popular music comes from the throat. Whether it is the falsetto scream of a heavy-metal vocalist, the wail of a blues singer, or the aching cry of a soul singer, it's the sound of voices releasing emotional cries too strong for the throats that release them. The producer Brian Eno describes this—and other sounds in pop music connected to recording mediums—as the sound of failure, of things going out of control, of mediums being pushed to their limits and breaking apart. These failures give popular music its sense of the transcendent, of things happening beyond perceived limits, and they might just be why popular music makes us feel so many things. Pop music is a vehicle for expressing the inexpressible, for what is beyond the limits in life.

Of course, even when guitar distortion led to the rise of bigger amplifiers, the desire for the sound of distortion didn't diminish. Instead, it became a defining element of electric guitar playing. With bigger amplification and recording technologies, distortion and other mistakes could be built into the system and thus contained. The sound of things going out of control is the sound of failure. Some try to address the distortion by reducing it, but others hear it as the sound of breakthrough, of new potential, of new iteration. Pop music is about failing in new ways, expanding, evolving, and breaking apart containers that are no longer able to its contain sounds.

21

Shoes

My green polka-dot chukka boots by Mark McNairy

Bono, the lead singer of U2, wears big shoes. It might have to do with his height. But it might also have to do with where he comes from. His footwear reflects his musical roots and associations. When I was growing up, he was well-known for wearing what we affectionately called brothel-creepers: slightly pointed-toe leather or black suede shoes with thick crepe soles. These shoes are rich in historical pop cultural associations beginning with the Teddy Boys and rockabillies and later the punks.

Bono's footwear of choice is linked to his band's musical roots and influences, shaped by bands such as the Clash and the Sex Pistols. U2 has always attempted, in its own much-contested way, to honor those roots in its music, speech, and dress. The sunglasses Bono affected as part of his pseudo-Elvis/Devil character Fly in the early years of U2's music represent the battle between a man and his inner rock star ego, all narcissistic and self-absorbed. You can tell a lot about people from the way they dress. It's a clue to where they are coming from—even when they pay no attention to it themselves.

Here's the deal with shoes. Many people get them wrong. Invest in them and buy good ones—strong, substantial soles that root you to the earth. No square toes, no Tevas, no Crocs, no sneakers as dress shoes. You're not Mick Jagger—and even he looks daft with his bespoke clothes and Nike what-the-fucks on his feet. If you need to wear trainers, plimsolls, tennis shoes, or whatever you call them, try Vans slip-ons or Converse All-Stars. Get them dirty. The rest are unnecessary, unless you actually are an athlete—then one should only wear them when participating in that sport.

Don't tell me you need comfort. Nothing is better than a great pair of shoes you have worn comfortable. Most shoe stores you visit have a limited supply of suitable shoes, so move right past the ones with bells and whistles (shoe game is a craft that takes time to master) and go for something smart and classic. Then wear them like you know what it means to have your feet on the ground.

Oh, and don't forget: never trust a man wearing square-toed shoes.

22

When Tokyo Was Still the Future: Why I Travel

You take delight not in a city's seven or seventy wonders, but in the answer it gives a question of yours.

—Italo Calvino

For as long as I can remember, I have been curious about the world. I like to get lost and I don't want what I can get at home when I travel somewhere else. I like what's new, what's different, what others might fear. I'm strange that way. I had an early childhood fascination with maps and other cultures, but it was a Jackson Browne song that really awakened my desire to travel.

From his 1972 debut album, the song "Something Fine" is a deeply emotional, almost melancholic exploration of the heart's longing and desire. Browne's lyrics describe him as caught between the past and future, love lost and love longed for. He mentions California, England, and Morocco as devices to anchor the wrestling in his heart. As much as the lyrics, the song's melody is severely important. The song is stripped bare and plaintive, like a siren song pulling me out of the mist into the wild polarities of a world of beautiful things.

The first time I heard it, this song was like a stamp on my

internal passport, evoking my own past and future. At the time, my homeland of England, mentioned in the song, was caught between an old establishment and a new Britain that began emerging in the latter half of the twentieth century. And then there were the dual images of California and Morocco: California was new and fresh like a love-hungry child, and Morocco was exotic, evocative, and mysterious. Those lyrics opened up the world to me, filling me with a desire to explore. I began traveling in earnest because of this song, and I still often play it before I'm about to go on another trip.

I love the sense of the exotic you encounter when traveling. Going somewhere so unlike your own homeland bombards your senses with sight and sound, color and smells—it's like an electric change. Exoticness means different things to different people, but to me it means being in a place that has something to teach you. That is why it's important to create your own list of places you find exotic—we are all enthralled by different things and those things should direct our travels. The internet is full of listicles of exotic places, but they may not strike you the way others do.

Because of Browne's song, California and Morocco became polarities for me—the new world and the old—and they taught me different things. California's constant sunshine and culture built on dreams spoke to the creative parts of me and helped me break out of a tendency to limit myself. Africa, so unlike anywhere I've ever been, taught me the different ways people shape their lives and communities. It showed me the resilience of humanity in the face of hardship and struggle.

Travel opens us up to newness, difference, and otherness. I'm not someone who needs to find English food or the comforts of home when I travel. I'm not saying creature comforts aren't important, but I like the challenge of navigating a new environment. Travel has helped me with my shyness, forcing me to look people in the eye and find a way to communicate, breaking out of my almost pathological shyness and timidity. "You don't ask, you don't get" is one of my rules of travel. Travel makes you humble and vulnerable, but I have found this to be a gift rather than a curse.

Travel gives us perspective. This is when travel becomes pilgrimage, I think. The distinction between travel and pilgrimages has to do with the nature of the journey. Both travel and pilgrimages aim to arrive somewhere specific, be it a city or a religious site. With travel, destination is the focus. But with pilgrimage, the journey itself matters just as well.

A few years ago, I had an idea to undertake some journeys with a group of friends. Like with a pilgrimage, on this trip it occurred to me that rather than traveling to a specific place, it was the nature of the place that mattered. In the Bible there are three places of pilgrimage, locations where people traveled to have some kind of encounter: mountains, deserts, and waters. These three topographies shaped how understanding was offered to people. Moses climbed a mountain to meet God, Jesus spent forty days in the desert, and John the Baptist stood in the Jordan River and called people to be cleansed.

So, we took three journeys across California: to the mountains, to the desert, and to the waters. Each place represented something different. The mountain experience was about perspective, the grand view above the world where we could see things in a different way. Mountains are often where people go to get revelations from God. Desert journeys tend to be focused more inward. The desert's emptiness and lack of external stimulation takes you inside yourself, where you can wrestle with your demons and face yourself in self-awareness. And waters are places of transition and rebirth. Water invites us to a sense of newness; it helps us cleanse ourselves and leave things behind—our dead skin, our filth. It washes away the grime of existence and quenches our thirst.

After first hearing "Something Fine," the first place I went was

Denmark. I went with a friend to find a girl we'd met. From there, I hitchhiked to Greece and spent the summer on a nude beach in Corfu. I went to Tokyo for the first time in the 1970s, back when it was still the future of the world. Everything about it felt alien, yet like home. Years later, I was shooting a TV show in Moscow when a group of communist hard-liners staged a failed coup against Mikhail Gorbachev's reforms. And then I traveled the world with a rock band.

I have been on many trips, some short, some long—adventures, retreats, holidays, explorations. I don't have a bucket list; why put a limit on where you might go?

Some say the most important journey is the one within. I say it's to whatever airport will take you where you want to go next. You can do the inner work on the way.

23

Orvieto

I recently took a group of students to Italy for a couple weeks. I was teaching a class on the medieval period and technology, exploring ways in which culture shifts and how the Middle Ages still inform the way we look at the world today. We stayed in a monastery in Orvieto, a beautiful city halfway between Rome and Florence. In the center of the town is a beautiful church whose cornerstone was laid by a thirteenth-century pope.

On the first day of classes, we explored the city with the task to use all our senses and then write a poem about what we discovered. Everyone was to touch, taste, smell, and look at the city. This is what I wrote:

Layers of history slide
Beneath my soft skin
Touching the hard edge of ages
Volcanic ground beneath my feet
Supports yet one more pilgrim
Ancient truths inscribed in ochre
Picasso-striped cathedral
Once proud, now struggling
Gray against a sky that
Moves faster than time
Coughs and splutters
Espresso machines kick into life

The sound of a million heartbeats
In one cup

At the end of our stay, I took everyone across the town and into the old medieval quarter, where few had yet ventured. In that quiet part of town was a little church called San Giovenale, first built sometime in the late ninth or early tenth century. It was rough around the edges, various renovations evident in its clashing bricks, stones, and faded frescoes. But it had a magic feel.

At the church, I talked to my students about art, technology, and the relationship between the past and the future. I talked about not letting the past hold us hostage, as if God is more interested in it than the present. Ghosts of the past become a tyranny that hold the present ransom to ways of thinking, being, and doing that no longer resonate. And, finally, I told them a story about San Giovenale.

Long before Christianity found its way to Orvieto, it was an Etruscan town. A temple had been erected at the very site upon which this church now stood, and it was dedicated to Jupiter, the god of sky and lightning. As old as this building was, something older was in the soil beneath us. It was the ancient human desire to mark life and make it sacred, to dedicate a place and themselves to the gods—those we construct and believe in, those we love and serve, those we fear and worship, who haunt and cajole us, and who ache and bleed for us. San Giovenale is one among many Christian churches and cathedrals built on the site of older religious structures. We build upon the sacredness that has gone before us, I told my students.

Author Karen Armstrong has said that whenever humans experience a technological shift, they change their ideas about the divine and the human. Along with it shifts our consciousness and we come to new understandings about ourselves and about the sacred. San Giovenale sits in a spot that for centuries has held the lives of many people in its arms, so sure they had a corner on the truth, so confident in their understanding of how it all works.

But many years and technological shifts later, the building held a different message for us. We had learned to hold things lightly, to walk softly in the sacred places, and to be aware that what we know is really just how much we don't know.

PART III

Art: The Creative

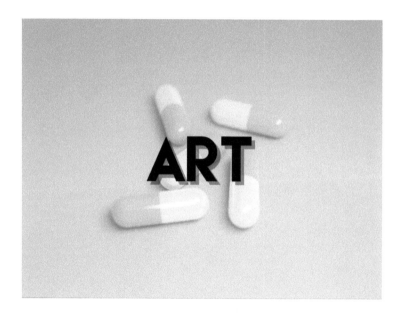

24

I Missed Punk, but I Got the Message

A punk-influenced art piece I made

I was on the road in America with AC/DC in 1976 when punk pierced the surface of British cultural life. It had been rumbling for a bit; record magazines were full of articles about this new movement, but nothing much had changed in the musical lives of my friends.

Music had built my youth: bands, whether comprised of friends or idols, and whether seeing them in concert or playing in them. I hung out with a group of musical people, most of whom were older than me and lived in a village near my home-town in a converted Victorian mansion called the Holme. Flat 4—essentially a rehearsal space—was the epicenter of the build-ing, as well as the music that emerged around the town. Nobody in the other flats seemed to mind the constant noise in the unit because most of them were in or connected to the bands that played and practiced there.

My friends' musical influences were broad, but American music, particularly from the West Coast, had worked its magic on us. A local musician and friend of ours had gained some suc-cess and moved to California to pursue his career. Occasion-ally, he would return to our area, sometimes in the company of his American friends, so part of the musical stew that evolved around us included his brand of UK-based blues and California harmony. The Beatles loomed large for some of us, as did soul music. Bob Marley was big, as were the Eagles, Fleetwood Mac, and Crosby, Stills, and Nash.

While I was crisscrossing the US with AC/DC, Britain was a cauldron of political frustration and social tension. There were strikes and protest marches. Unemployment was high. London stunk to high heaven because of a months-long trash strike. And troubles in Ireland had spilled over into the UK mainland. Most of this was lost on me as I journeyed around America, focused only on getting to the next gig on time after yet another four- or five-hundred-mile overnight drive.

Life as a roadie is nothing if not obsessive. All that matters is what your band is doing. You don't become one of the biggest bands in the world if you are distracted or unfocused. Every day you know what is going to happen and, more importantly, why it needs to happen. Of course, there are perks to this relentlessness, but it's a small, self-contained world.

This was also the era of pre–digital technology. We didn't have cell phones, and we had barely any contact with home except for the occasional pay-phone call or postcard. My time in the US was supposed to last for a few weeks, but it turned into months because the band started to break big. So, we kept going. We kept making tour plans that were scrapped almost overnight as things moved faster. One weekend, we went from Omaha, Nebraska, to the Netherlands for a TV appearance, and then to Miami, Florida. It was fantastic. Tiring, sure, but fantastic.

Eventually, we all needed a break and I got to go home for the first time in ages. What awaited me was mind-blowing. When I had left, most of my friends were in a late-1970s hippie phase. Long hair, jeans, nothing particularly forward-looking, fashionwise. But when I returned, I was greeted by a bunch of punks. Everything had changed: the dress, the music, and the attitude. Suddenly, the center of the musical universe had shifted from the US, which had always held the top spot among my friends. We may have had the British invasion, but all those bands—the Beatles, the Stones—they started out playing American music. But punk was something else.

Punk was perhaps the most significant thing ever to happen in youth culture at the time. It formed in our era's crucible of disappointment and frustration. It was music that raged against the machine, using urgency and creative dissent as its weapons. Punk was a confrontation with orthodoxy, a moral cleansing movement. Its musicians were heretics who dared to believe you could pick up instruments you could barely play, make some noise, and be a band. Punk was a critique of the bloated, self-satisfied, indulgent music business, and a rallying cry for those disaffected by the unfulfilled promises of the modern world. The late 1970s, specifically 1977, signaled the end of the future and the modern world. Punk was a sign of a generation's loss of faith. "No future!" it sang.

Punk's subcultural status meant it could explore sexuality without much attention. David Bowie was already working at that coalface, offering up a new vision of what it meant to be a man in the post-countercultural world of the 1970s. But punk rock was the first genre in which women were given equal ground. The Slits, Siouxsie and the Banshees, and X-Ray Spex were every bit an integral part of the punk scene as the Sex Pistols or the Clash. Nobody cared about your gender or who you had sex with. For many punks, sex was employed as a shock tactic against the conventions that held sway. Punk was anti-hippie and anti–free love, ideas that still hovered around youth culture in the wake of the late 1960s.

Inspired by the Situationists (precursors to the postmodern philosophers), punk practiced subversive tactics, particularly in its wardrobe. T-shirts with slogans, ripped and torn clothing, safety pins—it was all political commentary, a reaction against commodified youth culture. The streets are full of trash, so wear a trash bag. Society confines you to the margins and gives you little hope of access to its version of a good life, so create your own and live by a different set of rules. Homemade became the hallmark of punk. It was the first genre of rock music to produce its own magazines en masse. Gig posters, clothing, recordings—all of it was DIY, lo-fi, and against the market stream.

At the height of punk, I helped a friend do stage work on a short tour of Britain with X-Ray Spex. Like the Sex Pistols, the band released only one album, *Germfree Adolescents*, but it is central to the story of punk.

X-Ray Spex had a different lineup than the traditional bass, drum, and guitars of most punk bands. To that familiar setup, the band added a saxophone player. She was fifteen years old at the time, still at school and learning to play the instrument, but musical ability was secondary to the whole ethos of punk. So Lora Logic, as she came to be known, wailed away on her sax and became part of the band's distinctive—terrible—sound.

They were not good musicians and they had very little stage presence, except for frontwoman Poly Styrene, who was a force of nature. But none of that mattered to their hordes of fans. Bands and fans relate to each other differently in punk music—or they did in the beginning. Punk bands were totems around which the fans gathered. Most of the time they played in small venues, pubs, clubs, and dive bars, where fans would pack in tight against the stage. Being close to each other, collapsing the boundary between fans and band, was the dynamic of punk. The musicians were not there to be rock gods; they were there to tear those idols down and put a stake in the heart of slick, consumerist rock music.

There are a couple things to note about rock music. The first is the beat. Rock is a music of beats and grooves. That's where most of it begins. Whether it is the backbeat of the Beatles, the disco hi-hat, the heavy-metal four-on-the-floor, the hip-hop drum machine, or the dance grooves of pop, it is all about the beat. The other notable element of rock is its gestural art form. Just like the visual art counterpart, in which paint is applied in broad, sweeping gestures, rock is all about emphatic gesture. The sneer of Johnny Rotten, the raised middle finger of Johnny Cash glaring at the camera, Robert Plant's primal scream, David Bowie's androgynous Ziggy Stardust—rock music is as much about the gesture as anything else. Each band of each musical subculture has its ritual signs and symbols. They are liturgical actions that signal and invite the faithful into the community.

All too often those gestures are misunderstood or viewed through an already biased and distorted lens. A few years back, I was invited to a church where the minister apparently knew a lot about rock music. I sat in the audience listening to him describe the satanic prayers AC/DC prayed before its shows, and he informed us that the band's name meant "Anti-Christ/ Devil's Children." That, as we say in England, is a load of old codswallop.

As far as I know, the band's name came from a vacuum cleaner, complete with the lightning bolt in the middle, alerting Australian users to make sure they plugged the appliance into an alternate current rather than a direct current socket. As for the satanic rituals. . . . If changing guitar strings, going over set lists, and worrying about sound quality constitutes a satanic rite, then we were all were deep in the grips of Satan. But if not, I think they were just a band playing music.

Lots of satanic accusations are made against rock music, and I'm sure there are people in the world of rock who actually do yield themselves over to dark stuff. But I never met a practicing satanist when I was on the road. Of course, that is not the sort of information one might easily volunteer, and the death metal genre is often more likely to openly profess atheist and satanic tendencies. Like most things, there is a lot of sensationalism at work in the link between the occult and rock music. It is rooted as much in rock's antiestablishment posture as it is in a desire for the dark side.

Take, for example, the raised "horn hand" of metal bands and their fans. The symbol is utilized by virtually every hard-rock band in existence and determined by some to be a sign of the devil. Nobody seems to know how it became such a pervasive symbol in the heavy-metal music scene, but it is ubiquitous. Some trace it back to an artist named Ronnie James Dio, who said it came via his Italian grandmother, who used it as a sign to ward off the evil eye. Whatever its origins, it now means simply, "I want to rock out and have a good time"—hardly a demonic desire.

I suppose I should address the lyrics and the potential demonic content of the lyrics of the band I worked for. I mean, they did have songs called "Highway to Hell" and "Hells Bells." Rock music is not a discursive language. Words in music don't function the way they do in real life. If we all went around singing to each other rather than conversing, the world would seem a very strange place and I doubt we would get much done.

Lyrics in popular music function as only part, not the total sum, of a song's meaning. Meaning also lies in the song's emotional arc, formed from all the pieces involved in its creation: bass, drums, guitar, vocals. That's why our reactions to and interactions with music are so subjective. Half the time it is hard to guess what the song even means if we break it down word by word. Or the meaning is so vapid that you wonder why you yourself can't write a millions-selling pop song and live richly off the royalties. Songs take you on a journey. They create a world, as Brian Eno says, and invite you in.

Listen to a singer such as Otis Redding, who can stretch a one-syllable word to its breaking point. His vocals arc and loop and bleed against the instruments as he pours out his heart. His words are reduced to an almost guttural cry—but you get it, because you feel that way too. That's the thing with popular music; it's about capturing an emotion. Music captures a range of human characteristics and wraps them in instrumentation, offering them back to you like a talisman. Certain songs are important and sacred to us because they are more than the sum of their parts. Bruce Springsteen recently said, "You can change a life in three minutes with the right song."

I approach my theological work from a musical perspective. I look for the melody, rhythm, and beat of Scripture and I try to grasp the emotional arc of what I find. There is little in the way of tangible information about lots of things in the Scripture. Many consider the Bible to be a manual for living, though it's a strange one because things aren't always clear. But the emotions are laid bare on the surface of the book. Trace Jesus's words through the Gospel of Mark and you will find that his anger, frustration, alienation, and loneliness are palpable. If you read it like a song—looking for rhythm, groove, and melody—you can actually begin to feel it.

On the wall of my home is a piece of homemade art comprised of a Sex Pistols flag and a few other bits of personal stuff. Around the frame I wrote a quote from Joe Strummer, the lead singer of the Clash: "Punk rock means exemplary manners to your fellow human beings." Punk may have been angry—and rightly so—but at its heart was concern for the misbegotten, the forgotten, and the marginalized. It gave a renewed sense of hope to people locked in suburban lives with limited future. "Here's a way out. You are not alone," it said. It was solidarity in frustration.

Is it me or Johnny Rotten? newspaper clipping

25

Collage, Bricolage, Assemblage

I am and have always been a maker of art. I paint badly, and I draw just as well. I make sculptures and curio boxes out of found materials. But mostly I make collages. For the past twenty-five years, I've made one almost every day.

The habit developed out of journaling, something else I have done for most of my life. I used to write every day about the usual stuff: concerts and other events I've attended, frustrations, desires, quotes, and ideas—all the things you put down just for yourself. As time went on, I began sticking bits of ephemera alongside my writing, like ticket stubs, wrappers, odd things I picked up in the street. Then I began drawing in them as well. Journaling was a calming way of reflecting on my life. One day, I decided I wouldn't write. Instead, I created a collage. I'm a magazine junkie, particularly art and fashion magazines, so I had plenty of images to work with. When I finished the collage, I tried to write on it, but the glue hadn't dried and the pen wouldn't write. Instead, I cut letters out of a magazine and reduced my day down to three of four things: work, dinner with so and so, art class, whatever. The exercise captured the essence of my day with a few images and some cut-out letters, and eventually this became my habit. Then I discovered Peter Beard.

Beard is an American photographer, artist, writer, and diarist. He lived in Kenya for a time, in a tent on property belonging to Karen Blixen, who is most known for her 1937 memoir *Out of Africa* and the film of the same name. Beard was a fashion and rock photographer who moved in New York art circles, but his diaries are what captured my attention. He keeps amazing diaries full of images, his own and taken from elsewhere, combined with all sorts of notes, ephemera, and hand-drawn figures. His African wildlife photography is world famous and commands huge fees. So do massive, blown-up images of pages from his journals, which he customizes at his gallery shows with hand-smeared blood, stones, snakeskin, and anything else he fancies. A friend once took me to an opening of one of his rare Los Angeles shows and I was blown away by his creativity. His work became an inspiration to my own art. So, I refined my collages by reducing the words and using found images and objects to capture my thoughts and feelings on any given day. I do it almost daily, and it is probably my most disciplined habit.

The term collage is said to have been coined by Pablo Picasso and his friend Georges Braque at the turn of the twentieth century, when collage was brought into the fine arts world. Picasso's 1912 piece *Still Life with Chair Caning* is the first example of collage in fine art. Although it has been around for a long time, collage has taken on a new level of significance since its inclusion in the processes and techniques of modern art.

Something about collage points to the fragmented reality of contemporary life. Many disparate things are forced to live side by side. In my own collaging, I seldom have a vision for what I want to make. I just let the random available images express what I feel.

Maybe that's what collaging is—dealing with the randomness of life. The iPod Shuffle first debuted with a similar purpose.

It was the first piece of software built for randomness and it became a metaphor for how to deal with the unpredictable and learn to live with what it brings you, for it will soon change to another song in a few minutes.

Bricolage is another French word that captures both a form of art and a philosophical theory. It essentially means "do-it-yourself" and is connected to the creation of an artwork or theory from a diverse range of available things. The term became popular among postmodern philosophers such as Jacques Derrida and Claude Lévi-Strauss. Strauss used it to describe a method of thought that opposes what he regarded as the mechanized thinking of the modern world, which was about ends and means. For him, bricolage involved using old materials and ideas to solve new problems.

A bricoleur uses whatever materials are available to generate new meaning in the world. Early twentieth-century art movements such as Surrealism, Dadaism, and Cubism all bear traces of bricolage. But it was in the 1960s that bricolage art took on a more political shape. Bricolage artists made sculptures and other pieces out of rubbish to criticize the art world's rampant commercialization. They made works out of everyday trash in hopes of asserting the value of the ordinary and devaluing the art object itself.

This same idea was explored in the early 2000s by British artists Sue Webster and Tim Noble, who created a series of sculptures from the trash they found in the neighborhood around their London home. At first glance, their sculptures simply look like piles of trash, mountains of things that characterize our throwaway culture. But the sculptures hold a second element. They are in fact precise constructions that can only be seen when light is shined on them, turning meaningless trash into meaningful shadows of people and other scenes from everyday life.

The artists used these sculptures to spotlight our complicity in trash culture, the small, daily ways we contribute to the world's litter and the increasing ecological challenges raised by our carelessness, all because of our love affair with the disposable. Their abstract sculptures require a close viewing and a willingness to look beyond darkness into light. Webster's and Noble's constructions signal that perhaps our own inventiveness and creativity could light the way to another way of living if we face the choices that we often leave in the dark. They are an invitation to consider that the clues and answers to a better way of living lie around us in the everyday, the ordinary, and the throwaway.

Good Friday, collage by me

26

Elvis's Belly

The music of Australian singer-songwriter Nick Cave has been central to my life, and so has his writing. In his 2015 book, *The Sick Bag Song*, so named because he wrote it on airplane sick bags, he writes about a song in which he conjures up an image of himself pushing Elvis Presley's belly up a hill, a reference to the myth of Sisyphus.

In this passage, he alludes to living with what he calls the burden of our influences. This is the shadow that falls across our lives in the shape of those we admire, follow, and seek to emulate. Cave has called himself king-sized in song, but ultimately he knows Elvis is the only real king in rock music. This passage is all poetic and tongue-in-cheek, but it does get at the idea of how we seldom transcend those who influence us, as hard as we might try.

Cave is one of my influences. You'd never know it, and I couldn't come close to his giftedness. But almost every time I pick up a guitar or think about a lyric, his image floats into my mind. I've been pushing him uphill for years. Other than AC/DC, I have seen Nick Cave in concert more than any other artist.

In 2004, I was standing at the bar in the back of the Brixton

Academy, a music venue in London, with my brother. Onstage, Nick Cave and the Bad Seeds were conjuring up music of epic proportion—wailing instruments and pounding drums, mania flowed off the stage like a fever and infected the audience. Stark white lighting threw long shadows of the band along the venue walls, making them look like vampiric creatures in an F. W. Murnau film. My brother, who is not known for his religious interests, leaned over to me and shouted, "Bloody hell, it's the house band in hell—or heaven!" He meant it in the most complimentary way. This music was transcendent, rapturous, a sound that only angels might make—if they were angels of the apocalypse, perhaps.

Cave has mined the Bible throughout his musical career, filling his songs with imagery drawn from its pages. Like Leonard Cohen, Cave has crafted a personal interpretation of Scripture. He once said that God lives in his songs but not outside of them. "Life is not a story. It's often one event piled on top of another event," Cave said in the lovely and poignant 2016 documentary *One More Time with Feeling*, which was released to promote *Skeleton Tree*, his latest album with the Bad Seeds. The documentary was intended as a buffer, a way of promoting the album without having to face the press in the wake of his fifteen-year-old son's tragic death. Making both an album and a documentary in the wake of immense loss is an accomplishment alone, but these two works are more than just admirable efforts at confronting life's tragic curveballs; they are perhaps the most honest and beautiful confrontations with grief I've encountered in a long while.

Skeleton Tree released in 2016 just months after David Bowie's final album, *Blackstar*, which came loaded with meditations on what turned out to be Bowie's own fast-approaching death. That year, pop music gave us rich tools with which to face mortality, works that resonated with deep honesty and offered no easy answers to life's challenges. You might think a film shot following Cave's immense tragedy would be voyeuristically morbid, but *One More Time with Feeling* isn't heavy-handed or leaden. It simply breathes and aches as you breathe and ache with it. The film hints at the tragedy from the beginning, but it draws us deeper and deeper into the film before telling that story. The film's 3-D effect might seem like an odd choice given its content, but the camera spirals through everything, gently drawing us into the heart of things. Its greatest gift is its offering of something rare in these days of platitudes and rehearsed answers to all of life's complexities: it faces grief in all its rawness, and doesn't overcome it.

Much like the writer Christopher Hitchens, who challenged the language of "fighting" cancer, Cave faces the loss of his son not by crying out to God or overcoming the demon of loss, emerging as the conqueror of grief. Instead, with candor and deep pain, Cave acknowledges that certain life events can change you forever. "Time has become elastic," he says. In healing from traumatic loss, you might stretch away from the event, but you can always snap back to that moment when your life changed forever. The challenge, Cave offers, is to remember that surviving such loss is about figuring out, again and again, how to live with the unfamiliar person it has turned you into.

Seven of the eight *Skeleton Tree* songs featured in the film were recorded before his son's death, but all of them are somehow weighted with the grief. The resulting work of art is a sublime meditation against the tragic unfairness of life. Toward the end of the documentary, each person featured in it is shown portrait-like against a gray wall—the film crew, the band, Nick's wife, his surviving twin son Earl, and then an empty frame—the portrait of a missing son. Cave's voice explains that he and his wife have decided to be happy as an act of revenge against death.

When tragedy strikes, we must find a way to live again—without answers, because there are none. Cave's path of revenge might just be the way to go.

27

Fallen Angels

Music has always been my church. I might go to buildings, participate in rituals, and even make a living by engaging with more traditional forms of church and religion, but in my heart, music is my religion. It was in music that I found a space to hear and voice my desire, melancholy, sexuality—everything. I remember, with a fondness I don't reserve for many things, when I bought my first record player. It wasn't the machine itself, but what it represented: liberation from the family sound system, from my parents' radio choices, from the tyranny of a world shaped by ideas, values, and aesthetics that meant little to me as I tried to voice my own. That record player became a shrine, a holy site at which to make incantations and supplications. I learned about life's pains, struggles, joys, and freedoms as the records revolved. I dreamed of a different life through blues, gospel, R & B, soul, reggae, punk, rock, and pop artists whose music became a soundtrack for my own.

Lately I've been reading *The Art of Nick Cave*, a 2013 collection of essays about Cave's music, writing, and influence, as well as the elements of the sacred and the profane in his work. Throughout his career, Cave has often used the Bible as an imaginative lens through which to invite us to look at the world.

In the book's introduction, editor John H. Baker reflects on Cave as an actor in the 1987 Wim Wenders film *Wings of Desire*, in which he plays Damiel, a fallen angel. Baker likens Cave's songwriting to the trajectory of a fallen angel whose fall is not to destruction but to empathy. According to Baker, the only way the angel can fulfill his desire is to undergo a radical shift or reincarnation of sorts. He risks, like Lucifer, a fall from the spiritual into the material world. For some who hold a different view of what it means to fall, this might be a troubling turn of events. But in the film and in Cave's music, the only way desire can be fulfilled and love can be realized is by falling to Earth.

Similarly, David Bowie plays an alien who is transformed by humans in Nicolas Roeg's 1976 film *The Man Who Fell to Earth*. The story is like Wenders's in that radical transformation occurs in the fall. The notion behind these falls is that desire and drive are not met by escaping reality or the material world, but by fully entering into it.

The forms of Christianity I have participated in for much of my life have always focused on escaping materiality. The religious eye is often inclined toward the heavens, rather than the Earth. But lately I have been dreaming that I am continually falling to the ground. At first I was worried—it felt troubling and I wasn't sure what, if anything, it meant. But I am beginning to see it differently, as an unconscious acknowledgment of shifts I have been making in life.

Many Christians understand faith as a set of beliefs about the world. We are good at reducing things down to religious affirmations. It's how we think we can determine who is in or out, who is with us, who is part of our tribe. But for me, faith is an expression of a type of life, a material one, an existence focused on this world instead of an otherworld. Christianity is an invitation to fall more deeply into the world, not escape from it. In this sense, every Christian is a fallen angel.

28

An Elegy for Leonard Cohen

The year 2016 was brutal for popular music. The musical canon of many artists is closing. They will give us no more songs, sing us no more melodies, and tell us no more tales. Now all we hold of them is their voices and their songs.

"I struggled with some demons/ They were middle-class and tame" ("You Want It Darker," lyrics by Leonard Cohen, 2016).

All hail the poet theologian Leonard Cohen, who sadly left this Earth.

All hail Leonard Cohen, who wrote eighty verses for his song "Hallelujah" dressed in his underwear, banging his head on a hotel floor.

All hail Leonard Cohen, whose songs wrap around you like a cloak, hiding you in the dark recesses of their melodies.

All hail Leonard Cohen, who spent years sitting in silence in a Buddhist retreat center, yet never considered himself a religious person.

All hail Leonard Cohen, who sings songs of things too deep to be spoken of.

All hail Leonard Cohen, the godfather of gloom, the grocer of despair.

All hail Leonard Cohen, who started a music career at age thirty-two.

All hail Leonard Cohen, whose credo was, "There is a crack in everything; that's how the light gets in."

All hail Leonard Cohen; he knew about life, and if you listened, you could learn.

All hail Leonard Cohen, who declared that the perfect and the broken hallelujahs have equal value.

All hail Leonard Cohen, whose demons are like mine: middle-class and lame.

All hail Leonard Cohen.

29

When Is a Painting Not a Painting?

One of my favorite artists is the New York painter Mark Tansey. Uniquely, his monochromatic works have an almost illustration-like quality. Tansey lays down a layer of oil-based pigment on the canvas, working a section at a time, a technique similar to that of Renaissance fresco painters, who applied only as much wet plaster as they could paint in a day. Then, with turpentine and found tools, which he calls his extended brushes, Tansey works backwards, removing the paint from the canvas with friction and erosion. He might use a ball of wool, a twig, or some crumpled-up lace—anything that will give the right texture to what he is attempting to draw up from the pigment.

Finding a tool that tactilely resonates with whatever object he is creating is like a game to him, he says. He might use pieces of crochet work to leave a visual impression of a tree, for instance. The finished works are dazzling and hard to walk away from. It's not simply the technique; it's the images he creates. He takes inspiration from photographs and magazine clippings to create collages from which he derives ideas for his paintings. Tansey also layers philosophical ideas into the works, sometimes by literally writing text into the painting, other times by using postmodernist and deconstructionist philosophy as inspiration and starting point for the work. To use these philosophical ideas, he created a cylindrical device on which he writes sentences and ideas and quotes and spins them around and from this gets a starting point for a new work.

His paintings appear, at first glance, to depict everyday or historical occurrences. But upon closer inspection, nothing is as it seems. Although his works could be considered realism, they aren't realistic at all. Tansey believes realism in painting was co-opted by the invention of photography, so he turned his attention to exploring how different realities interact. "I think of the painted picture as an embodiment of the very problem that we face with the notion 'reality,'" he once said. "The problem or question is, which reality?"

Which reality is a unique question for our time. The rise of neofundamentalism, nationalism, xenophobia, techno-fear, terrorism, global capitalism—these realities all meet in the tangled web of twenty-first-century life and in Tansey's works. Although the scenes he depicts have never actually occurred, they symbolically reflect how these new realities we live in interact and abrade. The abrasion, the rubbing away at the surface, takes place on two levels: in the process of the creation of the works and in the images themselves.

Tansey's painting *The Triumph of the New School* depicts two warring armies signing a peace treaty amidst a battleground littered with soldiers, weaponry, and battlefield dress. But on closer inspection, contradictions and paradoxes emerge. The soldiers on the left are dressed in the costume of the First World War, while the opposing army, with its tanks and guns, looks like American soldiers from the Second World War.

The painting reimagines a nonexistent moment in art history as a moment of battlefield surrender. The left army is the School of Paris, led by the founder of surrealism, André Breton, as its general. Pablo Picasso stands close by. The opposing general is none other than Clement Greenberg of the New York School, a famous modern art critic and representative of the American Abstract Expressionists. The moment Tansey portrays is the shift of the modern art world's axis in the 1950s. New York became its center as Europe surrendered to the triumph of modern artists: Willem de Kooning, Robert Rauschenberg, and others.

In the painting, these two schools of art sign a détente agreement, underlying which is a gulf of cultural difference captured in the French soldiers' formal dress and the Americans' more casual manner. The clothes suggest the cultural divide that is at the same time both real and not. In this work, Tansey creates a landscape in which the symbolic and the real exist side by side seemingly naturally, as if to say cultural shifts are constant.

There are some valuable theological lessons in Tansey's approach to his work. I am drawn to his use of subtraction as a means of creating. Rather than adding layers of paint onto a primed canvas, he scrubs away at it to tease out his images. This is akin to the philosophical notion of deconstruction. It's a radical theology idea of getting down into the roots, into the depths of the event of God, to tease out new conceptions of the sacred.

Deconstruction is often spoken of as a threat—tearing down something that already exists and is loved—but let's not confuse it with destruction. Destruction lays waste to things, and deconstruction does otherwise. Jacques Derrida, the philosopher most commonly associated with deconstruction, once explored the relationship between text and meaning by reading texts closely to see what in them might run counter to their intention. Deconstruction underscores the notion that whatever a given text is founded upon is complex, unstable, or impossible. That doesn't mean it has nothing to say; it just probably has more to say than we have allowed. We have failed to listen and let the text truly speak. Charges of relativism are often laid upon those who employ ideas such as deconstruction, but the opposite is true—it involves a close reading, not a disregard. Neither deconstruction nor radical theology is "dancing on the grave of God." Deconstruction invites a close reading in attempt to let the text say new things. And those new things might speak to new realities.

Similar to deconstruction, radical theology seeks to uncover what has perhaps been lost, missed, or ignored. Some still connect radical theology to the Death of God movement that emerged in the middle of the last century, but what I speak of is a theology *after* the death of God, a theology of and for the twenty-first century. Radical theology seeks to go back to the roots (radix) and, like deconstruction, to reread religious texts closely, teasing out new permutations and exchanging old understandings for new possibilities.

Eschewing the traditional tools of a painter, Tansey creates his own to achieve his aims. This embrace of anything and everything in the service of his art is a potent notion for creating a multidisciplinary approach to theology that uses whatever we have on hand—whether it's sociology, philosophy, anthropology, or poetry—to break down the stranglehold that traditional approaches exert over the field. Art and theology are similar in this way. The danger, of course, is that institutional organizations can always exert their stranglehold on things, but you don't need their support or blessings to do your work.

Every term at the art school where I teach, I introduce my students to the Dadaist and Situationist movements that emerged in the first half of the twentieth century. They were both deeply political, poetic, and artistic movements that called society to account for the absurdity of its ways. The Dadaists rejected ideas of reason and logic, particularly the aesthetes that drove the arts communities, in favor of nonsense and irrationality. They created sound poems, music, collages, and cut-up writing (David Bowie used the latter to generate many of his lyrics). With their absurd ideas and practices, they critiqued war, violence, and capitalism.

The Situationists, who came later (and influenced the UK punk movement via two of its earliest architects, Malcolm McLaren and Vivienne Westwood), were perhaps even more politically focused. Their sights were aimed firmly at capitalism. Guy Debord, who wrote *The Society of the Spectacle* in 1967, was a key member of the movement. At its heart was the notion of the spectacle, referring to mass media and the increasing control it exerted over people's lives. Situationists believed people were at the mercy of technology and consumption and were being lulled into a passive, unhealthy state.

The movement was also concerned about the expanding tendency for social relationships to be forged and mediated through objects and consumption. Situationists felt society had been infected by consumer capitalism, resulting in a growing sense of alienation. Like the Dadaists, they expressed themselves through art and music, and they pasted posters and slogans everywhere. They practiced subversive tactics, like filling newsstands with comic books that were rewritten to address their social issues of concern. They created situations to counter their own spectacle, moments of authentic unmediated experiences in which to experience life free from the media's gaze, influence, and control.

A final thing about Tansey's work: beware its absurdity. On the internet are lots of images of Tansey's paintings. If you spend time exploring, you might chuckle at many of them. A wry sense of humor infiltrates much of what he does, but sometimes it is so abstract that it seems simply absurd. And yet, if you linger with those works, exploring their various elements, you might find commentary, critique, and meaning. In fact, the absurdity of the works is what gives them the true weight of meaning.

Albert Camus famously created the philosophy of existential absurdism. For Camus, life was absurd. It was absurd because of an incongruous juxtaposition between humans who seek meaning for their existence and a world that has no meaning. His life became about questioning and exploring this absurdity. Camus's antidote to this philosophical problem was suicide. If life is truly absurd, might it be the only rational response? He found no solace in religion, which he knew offered consolation to many, because he saw it as an illusion. The illusion was connected to God's existence or nonexistence. If God did not exist, then of course religion was meaningless. On the other hand, if we were to discover proof God did exist, the only conclusion is that, given the incredible suffering in the world, God was at best cruel and at worst psychopathic. God's existence would only make life more absurd.

What if Christianity is meant to be an absurd contribution to reality? To me, Christianity's goal is not to give meaning, or even a counter-meaning, to society's prevailing ideas. Rather, its goal is to point out the absurdity of how we live and to invite us to reflect on those entangled realities so we might find other pathways of being. The heart of Christianity is the cross, the death, and the resurrection of Jesus. It's absurd. In the face of the onslaught of reason and scientific rationalism, we have burdened ourselves with the task of marrying fact and faith when it comes to our religious conceptions. Perhaps we have forgotten the absurdity of the notion of the death of God's son.

Kierkegaard said that if we are to believe, then it can't be through reason but by "virtue of the absurd." Much of Kierkegaard's work explored the notion of the absurd. He posited that Job, the Old Testament character who lost everything in a game between God and the devil, was restored by virtue of the absurd. By this same virtue, Abraham, the father of faith, got his reprieve from having to sacrifice his son Isaac.

All of this is to say, the absurd has been applied to Christianity before. We just seem to have lost sight of it in our hunger to be relevant and match science or other competing ideologies punch for punch. But at its heart, the story we have to tell is completely, well, absurd. Perhaps even more absurd is to continue attempting to make meaning out of Christianity and God. My remedy is to listen to Bob Dylan's classic song "With God on Our Side." Seven minutes and nine seconds is about all it should take to cure you of that notion.

Inspired by the Situationist practice of subverting comics, I post one of the Jesus Says cartoon strips on my Instagram (@ukbloke) every day

30

Twombly

In the 1950s, Cy Twombly was ascending to his status as a leader in the burgeoning New York art scene. This was the age when the art world's axis of power was shifting from the old world to the new. But at that moment, Twombly made a surprising move: he packed up and moved to southern Italy. Just as the spotlight fell on the emerging art scene in which he was a central figure, he chose obscurity and spent the rest of his life secluded in Italy.

There, he honed his style and found a voice of his own. One discipline he practiced was drawing in the dark, working for hours each night. He picked up the idea from the Surrealists, who practiced what they called "automatic writing." Twombly's intention was somewhat different—he was trying to undermine his confidence in his abilities, surrendering what he knew of drawing to the blindness of night. He wanted his lines to be softer, less certain, like a child's but without being childish. This was so he could better express his ideas when it came time to put them on canvas.

His work is not easy on the eye. He is one of those artists of whom some might say, "My kid could do that." Of course, a child could never—children don't have much awareness or substance beneath what they draw, but Twombly had it in spades.

Influenced by the old art world of Italy, Twombly's work responded to the ancient Greek and Roman art and architecture that surrounded him. The disparate history of graffiti on ancient walls also inspired his canvases. Twombly's paintings are rough, encrusted with layers of thin, sometimes barely decipherable, words scratched into the paint. He was layering time, collapsing the history of the art world into all his pieces. He blurred the lines between the old world and the new world, a line art critics loved to cultivate.

Critics, like the rest of us, love to draw dividing lines between ideas. Twombly, living in his own chosen exile, trampled over that line as if it never existed. He was fascinated with writing and language, and he was one of the first to incorporate text and graffiti-like writing into his paintings. This laid the foundation for generations to come, a heritage picked up particularly by Jean-Michel Basquiat, whose work echoes Twombly's wordplay as a means of toying with the viewer's interpretation. "I cross out words so you will see them more," Basquiat once said. Doodles, splotches, scrawls, and scratchy text all combine in their art to create immense works that are at once ethereal and heavy, erotic and ephemeral. They are paintings a child could do, if they had centuries of art history beating in their heart.

> To make lines less certain to practice vulnerability.
> To incorporate the past and the present to give shape to the future.
> To create childlike but not childish works.
> To play with words to create new meanings.

31

Bowie and Me

"Fuck!" wrote my friend Kester to me in a direct message on Twitter. It was January 2016. Something bad had happened, and it was this that would finally get me writing. I am a procrastinator of the first order; despite my best attempts, I remain firmly in the camp of "Wait until the last minute." I'm thinking all the time, but committing things to paper—well, that's another matter. But that Twitter message, like so many other small moments in my life, triggered something in me.

It was late when the message arrived. I was on my way to sleep but had forgotten to turn off my phone, and the ping of the message snapped me back to consciousness. "Fuck!" was all the message read. I didn't know what he meant, but it woke me up. I texted back, and within seconds came the words "Bowie's dead." I was stunned. Fuck, fuck, fuck.

I'd spent the whole weekend listening to *Blackstar*, David Bowie's latest album that had released on his sixty-ninth birthday two days prior. It's a stunning collection of songs, showcasing the man at his most adventurous and creative. Bowie's music has always been key to the soundtrack of my life, and I wasn't ready for his newest offering to also be his last. I opened up my record player, put the album on, and cried. I cried over the loss of someone I never met, but whose life impacted mine profoundly. With too much nervous energy, too much sadness coursing through my body to go back to sleep, I started writing.

Music for me has been a lifelong ritual of devotion. I still search for sounds and feels and grooves, and I still get giddy when the lights go down and a band hits the stage. But as a teenager, I was a music fundamentalist, living in a narrow-minded world of musical preference. It was a good world, but it was small. I was a soul boy, raised on the Kings: B. B., Albert, Ben E. The blues was my starting point, and gospel, R & B, and soul were the trajectories. I was a disciple of Curtis Mayfield, an acolyte of Little Stevie Wonder, and a devoted follower of Aretha Franklin. My choirs were the Staple Singers, the Clark Sisters, and every other vocal group from the Four Tops to the Chi-Lites, and I religiously worshipped at the altar of Donny Hathaway. I was a music snob. I never gave the Beatles, the Stones, or anyone else a chance. I gave Van Morrison an occasional look, because he too was a soul man, hacking away at the coalface of life armed with the Caledonia Soul Orchestra and a pocket full of Jackie Wilson and Wilson Pickett. My preferences were judgmental and opinionated, and I was ignorant of the wide world of music around me.

All that changed after I went to a party. It was somewhere in London, a hallway in a house party, that I encountered the sound of the future. The rest of the details are foggy, but I vividly recall walking down a hallway and hearing a sound blaring from the record player in the living room: Bowie's "Suffragette City." Since then, his music has provided much of the musical backdrop to my adult life, and his person and his songs provided the support and the impetus for some major life changes I have made. But why Bowie?

Bowie was to me like the Beatles were to the generation before. He signaled a shift, a movement in the cosmos, a point of departure from what had been. He was perhaps the perfect foil for life in the 1970s. Any giddiness leftover from the 1960s had long dissipated and Bowie came to the fore while social disillusionment gripped the nation. The swinging '60s gave way to the more sober and desperate '70s, and Bowie's sounds of dissonance, disconnection, and frustration were just what we needed.

Bowie invited us to join him in a whole new world, where he resisted society's dominant norms. The 1960s might have advocated free love, but Bowie pushed for a different collapse of boundaries. Playing around with his sexuality and appearance, he was queer before queer was a public idea. Wrapped in a homemade spacesuit or wearing theatrical feminine clothing, Bowie pushed the boundaries of what it meant to be male in 1970s Britain. We loved him for it, and he loved us back. For me and thousands of others like me, locked up in our boring English backwater existences, wracked with confusion and angst and a thirst for something, he told us we were not alone, that we were wonderful.

Every album in his decades-long creative journey was a revelation. Not every one was great, but you learned to live with his experiments. Bowie was not an artist prone to repetition. Like the rest of us, he had that late modern restlessness, characteristic of life in a world unmoored from its past and uncertain of where it is headed. That's the thing about Bowie—he didn't seem like us at all, but deep down we could sense he was. He put his restlessness into a ceaseless exploration of possibility in music, always pushing ahead whether in or out of favor. With his numerous alter egos—Ziggy, the Thin White Duke, Major Tom, Aladdin Sane—he was multiple personalities, each staking out new musical horizons.

Mark C. Taylor has said that religion is most interesting where it is the least obvious. One of those least obvious places might well be in the music of David Bowie. I doubt many people would describe Bowie's music as such, but I think notions about God have been in it since the start. "I realize God is a young man too" is a line from a song on his 1970 album *The Man Who Sold the World*. Perhaps it is his duet of "Heroes" with Queen at the 1992 Freddie Mercury Tribute Concert for AIDS Awareness, after which he kneeled and said—out of all the things he could have offered in that moment—the Lord's Prayer in honor of those lost to the disease.

In a press release for his 2003 album, *Reality*, he wrote that he titled it thus to juxtapose an older understanding of the world with what he called the "new tangle" it's become. He was thinking about the notion that there is no ultimate reality anymore, that there are no absolutes left. "This reality that we live through, its basis is more an all-pervasive influence of contingency rather than a defined structure of absolutes," he wrote.

This is the new world Bowie wanted to discuss in the early years of the new millennium, already ripped apart by 9/11 and full of new complex realities. He saw our world in a whole new reality without the benefit of old gods to help us, because they are dead, and we have killed them. The challenge then becomes whether to collapse in the face of the harsh new reality or to resurrect old gods in the hope that they might bring comfort. Bowie's remedy was to forge ahead into a new reality, trusting life's contingencies rather than its guarantees.

At times, Bowie's music holds a prayer-like quality, much like the music of Tom Waits, Nick Cave, or Leonard Cohen. The prayers, if they can be called such, held within the structures of those songs are desolate, lamentation and yearning being their chief hallmark. Every once in a while, you wonder if Bowie isn't playing a mind game with you—after all, this is the man who said part of his job was to tell lies. But that was probably a lie itself, a means of deflecting any sense that he might have a handle on what's going on in the world.

If Bowie has any religiosity, it is well hidden within the folds of his music. What is clear, though, is his visual critique of religion as well as his use of biblical imagery, which continued right up to his death. In his last video, for the song "Lazarus," he is strapped to a bed with strips of linen covering his eyes and buttons like pennies laid over his sockets. As Lazarus is raised, the bed turns upright.

Many of Bowie's videos feature him or other actors playing some kind of cleric in a moral compromise, as if to say that true religion has been co-opted by pretenders and the pathways to the sacred have been blocked by religious corruption. Maybe I'm reading my own religious frustration into the content. Or maybe Bowie wanted to expose religion and the emptiness of contemporary life characterized by violence, consumerism, and the perpetual pursuit of happiness for what it is: obstacles to a deeper dimension of life. I don't know that Bowie would have termed that a spiritual desire, but I just might.

His album *The Next Day* appeared in 2013 out of nowhere after a ten-year hiatus. Released without fanfare or prior warning, it was a marvelous feat in this age of digital leakage, where everything is promoted in advance. The first single, "Where Are We Now?", was surpassingly nostalgic and mournful. The song reflects on Bowie's past and explores his mortality, one that no one expected to occur so soon after. In the video, Bowie is a "man lost in time" who is "walking the dead," say the lyrics. "Where are we now?" Bowie asks. It was a good question, reminiscent of Jesus, who asked the Pharisees if they had any idea what time it was. Asking those questions—What time is it? Where are we now?—opens the door to theological reflection that offers something to this post-absolute world that struggles with new realities while old ghosts find a way into the future.

One last thing about Bowie. In 1999, Berklee College of Music awarded him an honorary doctorate and invited him to give its commencement address. In his speech, he told the graduates that he realized authenticity was never going to be his strength, so he preferred thinking of music as a game of "What if?" This probably accounts for his ability to juxtapose incongruous ideas and create something magical that challenges the way things are. Bowie called himself a non-musician, saying that once he had gathered enough competency to transmit his ideas to other musicians, he had gone on a crusade to "change the kind of information rock music contained." He brought musical ideas from other genres into the heart of rock 'n' roll and made it work, leaving us wondering why no one had done that before.

This creative energy continued right up to the very end, when, on his sixty-ninth birthday in 2016, just two days before his death, he released *Blackstar*. The album was backed by a group of jazz musicians with whom he had never before recorded. It was a rock 'n' roll album made by intentionally avoiding rock 'n' roll.

Religion often refuses to take note of changes in how our society sees things. We shouldn't acquiesce to perceived cultural pressure or make changes just because others think we should. But all too often, religion fails to update its outdated and out-moded mythologies in the pursuit of power or control. In his book *Sexual Excitement: Dynamics of Erotic Life*, Robert Stoller's offered up a critique of psychoanalysis, which he said had rapidly moved from a "revolution to respectability to outdated mythol-ogy." Arguably Christianity has followed a similar trajectory and that is tragic. David Bowie's boundary-pushing life and music might just be an example of a way to rediscover the revolution-ary impulse at the heart of Christianity that seems to be currently locked up in outdated mythologies and ideas that no longer speak to our current situation.

Some life lessons from Bowie's music:

Practice "What if?"

Juxtapose incongruous pieces of information.

Live with the contingencies rather than chasing absolutes.

Do theology by intentionally avoiding the theological.

Find new conversation partners.

SOME SONGS JUST WRAP AROUND YOU LIKE A CLOAK AND THEY SPEAK OF THINGS TOO DEEP TO BE SPOKEN OF.

PART IV

Religion: The Spiritual

32

The Other Woman

There is another woman in my life whose story must be told, because it was two women—one I slept with, the other I met only in the pages of a book—who influenced the reframing of my life.

After my encounter with Comfort in San Antonio in the late 1970s, I quickly reverted to my usual place in the world of rock 'n' roll, but my head became increasingly elsewhere. It was the same internal restlessness I have felt throughout my life, but I was checking out of the world I'd been living in and actively looking for something else. I liked being on the road, but it was temporary. Something else, something indefinable, pulled at me from within.

The rush of being on the road with a band in its ascendancy is intoxicating. Every show builds on the previous one and the crowds get larger, the energy gets more extreme, and everything expands at a breakneck pace. When you find yourself in the middle of it all, it's hard not to be swept up in the excitement. I started out with AC/DC when it was just myself and two other guys working with them. We crisscrossed America, then the world, playing tiny clubs and opening big shows for Kiss, Aerosmith, and a host of other '70s rock bands. In a short space of time, as the band became popular, clubs became theaters, which became arenas, which became stadiums. I traveled all over, met amazing people, and had great times with a bird's-eye view of one of the world's greatest rock bands.

I am often asked what the people of AC/DC were like. They were great—that's the simple answer. Angus and Malcolm Young, brothers who formed the band, were singularly focused on their music. Angus spent most of his downtime doing three things: playing guitar, drinking tea, and smoking. He was almost obsessive in his love of Chuck Berry. Malcolm was someone you didn't want to mess with. The band was his life and he protected it like an angry bear. As the band's rhythmic drive and visionary leader, he didn't suffer fools gladly. Bon Scott, the lead singer, whose tragic death in 1980 almost ended the band, was one of the nicest people I have ever known. He was not without fault—his penchant for heavy drinking ultimately cost him his life—but in terms of people who are actually worth meeting, he was one of the best. Generous, kind, and extremely funny, Bon was always adding to the guest list people he'd met at a restaurant, bar, or the hotel. Phil Rudd, the drummer, was quiet, edgy, and prone to anger. We were close and roomed together in the early days. We would spend hours talking, and I learned that he came from a troubled background and was haunted by ghosts of the past. Cliff Williams was the band's second bass player, who replaced Mark Evans. Cliff was quiet, polite, and eager to make his way into the heart of the band. He was easygoing and the best-looking in the band—he did all right for himself with the ladies.

Like myself and most of us on the crew, the lads in AC/DC were working-class men, clawing their way out of one world and into another. All that mattered to them was playing live. Offstage, they were low-key. Like all of us, they had their quirks, but they weren't really "rock star" types—no prima donna attitudes or excessive demands. You probably could have passed them on the street without giving a second look. In terms of rock star excess, in the early days particularly, the crew was way wilder. But on stage, that was something else. They became this blisteringly loud and synchronized machine, creating a monstrous, primal sound.

Being on the road with a band is part military campaign. Everything worked out in exact detail—the crew, the equipment, the load-in, the load-out. But it's also like a circus, with strange characters everywhere brought together by their passion for music, but with different gifts—lights, sound, guitar, drums. You pull into a town and set up your "tent," then you put on a show that delights an assembled audience. I liked the band and the people I worked with. Given other work options, being on the road with a band is not a bad one: flying around the world, living without most of the rules and constraints people deal with in their daily lives—and, of course, sex, drugs, and rock 'n' roll.

For a couple years, being on the road was my life. My family was the crew and the band. We ate and slept together on tour buses and in hotels, we partied, and we worked. We built massive Scalextric tracks on hotel floors and raced electric cars into the early hours of the morning. We took drugs, drank, had sex, and did all the stuff everyone assumes rock bands do. We also worked hard while touring endlessly, putting on shows five or six times a week, traversing the globe—setting up, taking down, and moving on. Airports became our second homes; arenas and stadiums around the world became our workplace, and we lived virtually every night for the roar of excitement as the band hit the stage. It was consuming. I was hardly ever home, and I didn't care.

After a while, it becomes simply what you do for a living. The exciting aspects become familiar and you get a little jaded. It's Tuesday? Must be Tokyo. Yawn. You start to lose your enthusiasm for travel. You do your work, then sit around backstage waiting for the night's proceedings to begin. I found myself getting restless. My life looked just like it did before: I was still doing drugs, sleeping with girls, doing my work, but something was nagging at me. Along with melancholy, self-loathing seems to be my emotional baseline. But my self-loathing was peaking at ugly levels and I was starting to feel that I needed to be a better a human being, lay off the drugs, and reconsider the person I was becoming. I began questioning what I needed to change within me in order to feel differently about myself.

Where I come from, religious faith played a small role in the lives of my family and friends. We grew up in a world after God. The residual presence of the church, which in Britain was part of the mechanism of the state, held little promise for anyone and was largely regarded as an unnecessary, vestigial appendage. No one I knew had any religious faith, apart from my maternal grandmother. I went to church with her for a while in my pre-teen years. She was Anglican but didn't like the local vicar, so she had moved to the other end of town to the Methodist church. There, a tiny group of ancients clustered together in the church's cavernous space, which echoed as their voices praised a God few others in town believed in—and theirs was the "lively" place. All I remember of it is the squeaky foot of Mr. Lane, who managed the local gentlemen's clothing store. He tapped his foot while he sang, loudly squeaking out of time with the organ.

During this time, I joined the Boys Brigade. It was the Methodist version of the Boy Scouts, but with more religion. I joined because the Brigade had a marching band and I wanted to play the drums. Unfortunately, I wasn't told until I was in that I had to be around for a while to get to the drums, and that playing the bugle was a prerequisite. I didn't fancy being a bugler, so I didn't last long. I did like the uniform, though. But apart from my short-lived encounter with the Methodists and the religious veneer of a British school education, I had little interest there.

But here's a funny thing. At school, we had assembly every week; it was essentially a church service. We would sing a hymn or two and our headmaster, Mr. Wakelin, would give a sermon. He also prayed the same prayer every week—the prayer of Ignatius of Loyola—and I have never forgotten it:

Teach us, good Lord,
to serve you as you deserve,
to give and not to count the cost,
to fight and not to heed the wounds,
to toil and not to seek for rest,
to labor and not to ask for any reward,
save that of knowing that we do your will.

I never thought I'd have use for it, and I didn't remember it until it welled up from the dark recesses of my mind when I decided I was going to commit my life to something other than AC/DC and rock 'n' roll. But I'm getting ahead of myself.

The day I first bought a Bible, I was accosted by a group of Christians who were picketing the band's show. It was the Highway to Hell tour, and these people weren't happy about AC/DC being in town. I was dressed head to toe in black and a jacket emblazoned with the tour name and logo, so when I enthusiastically showed them my purchase, I understood their surprise. But that's the problem with religion or its practitioners, isn't it? They think they have a handle on how life works and how its problems can be fixed, but they contribute to the demise of the very thing they hold dear simply by being blinded by their presuppositions. I've done it myself, so I get how easy it is to fall into that trap.

With that Bible, I did what I had been doing with a lot of texts I had picked up on my travels: I scoured it for clues about how to live well, about how to be a deeper, richer, and kinder human. I wasn't initially impressed. Sure, there's all that brutal stuff in the beginning. As Nick Cave put it in his introduction to the Gospel of Mark, the Old Testament reveals a "maniacal, punitive God who dealt out to His long-suffering humanity punishments that had me drop-jawed in disbelief at the very depth of their vengefulness." Page after page was nothing short of mythic madness. But I kept reading, searching for the thing that seemed so potently alive to Comfort and her friends in San Antonio. I didn't want their religion, but I wanted something. Perhaps if I could find it, I could refashion into something that would help me live a different life.

The New Testament soon captured my interest. It was less of a struggle than the Old Testament, but a single story was a game changer for me. It was in the Gospel of Luke, a book replete with stories and encounters between Jesus and a restless humanity struggling to come to terms with itself. In the story, Jesus went to dinner at the home of Simon the Pharisee. I didn't know it then, but in this kind of encounter, hospitality was used as a tool for interrogation, all wrapped up in politeness and sanctimony. Jesus had been invited there to be checked out and called out, basically.

But then an intrusion changes everything. A woman crashed the dinner, and she was no ordinary woman—she was a prostitute. In this scene, profane invaded the sacred, dirty humanity violated the home of Simon, a man devoted to a religion of avoiding dirt and grime, particularly the human kind. She entered the room and all hell broke loose. She sobbed, she wept, and she fell at the feet of Jesus and washed them with her tears. Then she dried them with her hair and poured perfume over them. The dinner host was disgusted (disgust being a key motivator of much religious thought and action) and, in the manner of great storytelling, had his internal thoughts laid bare on the page: "When the Pharisee who had invited him saw this, he said to himself, 'If this man were truly a prophet, he would know who was touching him, what kind of woman she is. She is a sinner'"(Luke 7:39).

But it gets better. Jesus asked his host to answer a riddle of sorts, a story about debt forgiveness. The host responded with a begrudging answer and so set the stage for a lesson about the judgments we make in life. "Then he turned toward the woman and said to Simon, 'Do you see this woman?'" (Luke 7:44). There is more to the story, but that one sentence is so full of action that it grabbed my gut and made me feel that I had found what I was looking for. The drama of the moment came alive to me.

Jesus spoke to the Pharisee, but his body was turned toward the woman. "Do you *see* her?" he asked. How could you not? But the Pharisee couldn't see her, only his label for her. As Kierkegaard noted, once you've labeled someone, you negate them. The label blinds you to anything else about the person. To the Pharisee, this was not a woman but instead the sum of what she had been labeled: a sinner. She was not another broken bird dealing with the anxiety of existence, but a sinner worthy of nothing but judgment, condemnation, and rejection.

In the drama of that moment, something spoke to the ache within me. I didn't like the person I was becoming. Rock 'n' roll life creates situations of fast intimacy. In life on tour, we were always cutting to the chase, paring down to the barest essentials. There was little time for building connection, but people readily made themselves available to us. Lots of the sexual encounters were like that—there was no relationship, just pure primal sexuality. I wasn't happy about how easily I could move in and out of people's lives without much thought for them after the fact. It was not who I wanted to be. This story gave me clues about how I could shift the way I was in the world. Don't label, judge, or presume to know who a person is, because you don't know what's going on with them. Just be fucking kind.

Laurent de Sutter, in his book *Métaphysique de la Putain* (*The Metaphysics of the Whore*), says the prostitute is a figure of truth, the point where all truths of society intervene. Prostitutes bring sex, desire, economics, and morality together in a collision of flesh. The forbidden becomes a location for encounter within the depth of who a person is. That seemed to be the case in this gospel story. And it brought me to some truth and awareness of my own: it was time to move on.

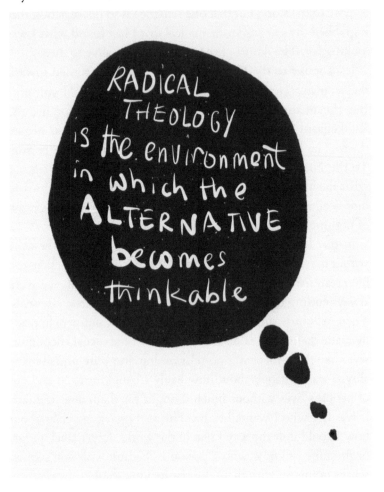

A thought cloud, iPad sketch by me

33

A Theological Life

What does it mean to be a theologian? It is a large part of who I am, but it was unplanned and unexpected. I often wonder just what it is I think I am up to. I'm still trying to be at home in religion, in life, in myself. I wonder if I have made any progress. Sometimes I feel I just keep digging a deeper hole for myself, my questions unanswered, my thoughts and ideas constantly changing.

Then I remind myself of Ludwig Wittgenstein's remarks about philosophy when defending it against those who saw little evidence of change. "If you scratch an itch, do you need to see progress?" he asked, implying that the task of philosophy is not so much to offer cures, but to scratch at the things that itch. I feel the same about the theological life: I'm scratching at the things that itch me. I don't need an end result or a fuller meaning to emerge from my questions. I have grown comfortable with a life absent of ultimate meaning and I thank theology for that.

I'm not a nostalgist; the theology I practice is of the present and the future. I like old ideas in much the same way I love old books—for their history, smell, feel, and connection with what was before. But I also scour the detritus of the current world for new clues, signs, and incantations. As Catherine Keller has said, theology is an "incantation at the edge of uncertainty." Some people might get nervous with the idea of theology as incantation, a sort of spell-casting. I take it to mean that theology uncovers the hidden possibilities lurking in an uncertain world where doubt reigns supreme. Theology's task in this environment is apocalyptic. It's a poetic revealing that opens up ambiguous pathways.

D. H. Lawrence said poets tear a hole in the firmaments and let some chaos in. Similarly, theologians are tasked with opening the safety nets people build with their beliefs and creating new space for expression. I came of age in a world where rationality drove theology, but that's not how I approach it myself. An incantation is an excess of words, language taken to its limits and stretched into something else to access something inaccessible. Like Otis Redding stretching his words into moans that make you ache with love and loss, an incantation is transgressive and transformative, and it invites the experience of transcendence.

That is what I mean when I say I am a theologian. I live at the edges of the world, digging around in the profane sacredness of life, casting spells and enchantments, and singing songs that need to be sung—songs of beauty and tragedy, pain and pleasure, losses and gains, love and hate. Songs of the gods who still haunt us and of the gods yet to come. Songs of the wonder of this meaningless existence riddled with meaning.

34

On Smugness

In 2011, preacher and author Lillian Daniel wrote an essay for HuffPost entitled "Spiritual but Not Religious? Please Stop Boring Me." Daniel addresses one of the major cultural dynamics at work in the twenty-first century: the divide between the religious and the spiritual. Daniel outlined what she regarded as naïve attitudes that come with faith on the spiritual side—the talk of sunsets and mountaintops and the lack of challenge that comes from having "deep thoughts all by oneself." While I appreciated her critique, I was struck by the smugness in all of this.

Late twentieth-, early twenty-first-century faith has developed significantly, particularly in the rise of neofundamentalism. September 11 and the ensuing upward trend of religious radicalism is considered a turning point that put religion firmly back in the public sphere, leading to new interrogations of religion by mainstream culture. While those discussions are often marked by negativity and naïve critique, this resurgence of interest in religion nevertheless hasn't been seen in Western culture for a long time.

The second issue is the rise of forms of spirituality that are characterized by hyper-individualism, which is often where the tension between religion and spirituality resides. Researcher George Barna once noted that while there are 310 million people in the United States, the danger is that we will wind up with as many versions of faith. So I understand Daniel's resistance. I used to live in Los Angeles, where spirituality, sometimes mad versions of it, can be found on virtually every corner. What is sometimes missed is the debt owed to the institutional religions. Individual spirituality is often influenced by ideas and practices held throughout the ages by the very religions people dismiss.

When Daniel's article came to me, the strangest part about it was that it was being passed around by people I know who view themselves as somewhat radical. But the real radical move is not to reject spirituality in favor of religion, but to reject both. Both are compartmentalized forms of faith and belief.

The chef and writer Robert Farrar Capon once said Christianity is neither a new religion nor even the best of religions; it is the proclamation of the end of religion. To him, the crucifixion is a sign that God is out of the religious business. I am not spiritual or religious—they both bore the fuck out of me right now.

35

A Shout

There is a scene in James Joyce's *Ulysses* where Stephen Dedalus, Joyce's alter ego, is conversing with Mr. Deasy when he "jerks his thumb towards the window" and says, "That's God!" When asked to explain what he means, with a shrug Dedalus declares God is a "shout in the streets." Perhaps for Joyce, the voice of God is nothing more than that of the people in the streets; the sound of heaving humanity is the only glimpse of God we might get. But to Dedalus and Deasy on the other side of the wall, God is an unexpected cry from the outside.

Deasy didn't recognize what Dedalus did; he didn't perceive God in the shout in the street. What if you don't hear the call? What if, for whatever reason, your ear is not attuned to the voice of God shouting in the street? I have encountered many people with whom the call or voice of God doesn't resonate. Traditionalists might argue that these people are willfully ignorant of God's claim upon their lives, but are they? History is full of people who never heard that call. What makes us hear it? And why at one particular time and not another?

How is it that someone such as Saint Augustine resists his mother's faithful urgings about his need of Christ and then one day hears a disembodied voice telling him to "take up and read," and in an instant he becomes the very person he had resisted for so long? Can a life possibly turn on such a dime?

I am hesitant to reduce religion, and Christianity in particular, to beliefs of this and not that. I have very little idea about what I believe, and working out my true beliefs is complicated. But I don't believe Christianity is meant to be about the intellectual assent to a bunch of propositional ideas about God. The philosopher Richard Kearney wrote that we can only begin to recover some sense of the sacred in ordinary life if we "concede that one knows virtually nothing about God."

The poet W. H. Auden wrote about the difference between what he called "believing still and believing again," or a naïve belief versus a tested one. Auden also understood Christianity as essentially derived from the commandment to love one's neighbor as oneself. I'm tempted to agree with psychoanalyst Jacques Lacan, who pointed out the irony of this commandment, as most of us actually hate ourselves. Or perhaps we could consider the inverse and say that given how we often treat each other, we have always loved our neighbors as ourselves, with the same level of disregard and cruelty.

In Auden's notion of Christianity, religion manifests in an obligation to other human beings, one rooted in this world, not focused on some other world that may or may not exist. In this world, life *before* death is the focus, not life after it. Auden's views might be anathema to many Christians. He eschewed supernaturalism, dogma, and doctrinal orthodoxies—things central to practicing a life of faith, rather than holding a system of beliefs.

But what if everything we have thought about religion is not how we should think about it now? What if Jesus was inviting his followers into a life of love that transcended all other ethics, moralism, or dogma? What if faith is not a set of beliefs, but something only found when we give ourselves to the world, when we embrace each other in the midst of our imperfections, with no goal other than to love?

While Oscar Wilde was imprisoned in Reading Gaol, he wrote what came to be regarded as one this most beautiful works, *De Profundis*. It was based on Psalm 130, which begins, "Out of the depths I cry." *De Profundis* was the work of man broken by harsh prison life and hard labor, but also broken by his awareness that his ego had ruined him. It's a deeply religious work, but Wilde's is a different kind of religion. He yearns to create a "confraternity of the faithless," an order for nonbelievers. Wilde did not find traditional religion in prison, but he found something else hidden in the depths of Christianity: himself. Wilde became himself in prison through a sort of aesthetic encounter. "Christ is just like a work of art," he wrote. "He does not teach one anything, but by being brought into his presence one becomes something."

The task before us is to reinterpret religious traditions—not to weaken or undermine their wisdom, but to renew them in the face of the new situations humans find ourselves in. We live in a world with no outside echo; transcendence has been pushed to the margins, and we can no longer simply appeal to the divine. Humanism is the dominant narrative of our world. I doubt the best response is a form Christian humanism, but just maybe, a radical, materialist Christianity might offer us hope.

36

Between Carnival and Lent

Around the middle of the sixteenth century, Pieter Breugel, the Flemish painter renowned for his portrayal of medieval life, painted *The Fight between Carnival and Lent*. Like many of his works, the painting captures everyday life in medieval Northern Europe, but also symbolism and commentary on events occurring in this world. This painting portrays tension between Protestants and Catholics over how best to reflect a meaningful spiritual life. The center of the town is filled with all kinds of people engaged in work and play, and around the edges two groups compete in a jousting contest. On one side is a group of people eating, drinking, gambling, and generally engaging in licentious activity. They are led by a jolly man astride a beer barrel. The opposing side is emerging from a church, led by a thin, witchlike nun holding a bread shovel upon which are two dried fish. She is followed by a host of penitents—nuns, monks, and townsfolk of all social levels, as well as civic leaders. They all appear mournful and downcast.

The painting highlights a particular theological battle of Breugel's time. It was in the early days of the Reformation and the battle lines between Protestants and Catholics were being harshly drawn. The conventional wisdom was that Protestants cared little for penitence and so celebrated Carnival and all its permitted excess, while Catholics opted for the ascetic avenue of Lent to express their devotion and loyalty. To this, Breugel offers a visual response. In the very center of the painting, we see a couple walking away. The man has a hunchback, which is said to symbolize egotism. It was often used as a symbol or representation of the way people cause intolerance toward dissenters for lack of thinking objectively. While he stands for man's own faults and weaknesses, the woman with him has an unlit lantern hanging from her belt. The pair are led by a fool, who carries an unlit torch, which symbolizes dispute and destruction. Close to the trio is a rooting pig, which often represents destruction and damage. All this division, Breugel says, is folly. Everyone in this battle is a fool.

In contemporary Christianity, Carnival doesn't get much consideration; in fact, it is largely regarded as a secular opportunity to dress wild and go crazy in the streets. But Carnival in Rio de Janeiro or Mardi Gras in New Orleans have little connection to religious life for most people, particularly those in the Protestant Church.

If there were a fight between Carnival and Lent today, Lent would win, hands down. Looking at the religious landscape, Lent is on the radar everywhere you turn. Lenten practices such as Ashes to Go and all kinds of alternative study groups are commonplace. And few religious people speak about Carnival. Sure, there is an occasional Shrove Tuesday nod to pancakes and celebration before the solemnity of Lent in some church circles and a few public pancake races, but no broader embrace of that liminal space where all bets are off and decadence and license run free. The Lenten dynamic is penitential, reflective, and internal—worthy aims, perhaps. But if they are not tempered by an embrace of life's wilder and external elements, I think we lose something.

Perhaps it's that Lent requires less effort. It's easily adapted to forms of faith that have become increasingly personalized over the past centuries, and many people look for rituals around which to order their lives. We also talk a lot about what we are giving up for Lent, something never meant to be an act of purely personal self-sacrifice. It has become a religious version of a New Year's resolution.

I'm not saying Lent shouldn't be observed; many people use it as an opportunity to intensely focus on or study something they haven't found time for. But something is being lost along the way, and living a bit more wildly might not be a bad idea. Lent has developed into a form of piety characterized by penance, by an interest in the cult of the martyrs, and by holding on to the vestiges of a past that has all but passed away. Back then, the church reacted to the problems of the age by advocating an ascetic approach to life, but in this modern age, a life of withdrawal is no longer what our culture necessarily needs.

Buddhist writer Pema Chödrön said the difference between theism and nontheism doesn't center on whether one believes in God but rather on how one views life. The theist believes they have a hand to hold, provided they live the right kind of life. Nontheists "relax with the ambiguity and uncertainty" of life without reaching for external protection. It might be more complex than that, but I like the way she changes the subject from a pointless debate on believing in God. The God thing is a set of ideas that is more complexly connected to our understanding of ourselves and how we confront our humanity.

I remain convinced that religion functions largely as a coping mechanism. The church's liturgy, be it traditional or otherwise, is filled with language that places God over humanity's affairs—guiding, loving, nurturing, caring. There is nothing wrong with that; we all need places to find peace or comfort. But when those notions break down, which they do, those conceptions become dead weight.

A few years ago, Bruce Springsteen said we must learn to

live with what we can't rise above. This might run counter to most conventional wisdom, which is riddled with the language of overcoming and triumph, but some things are not overcome and must be lived with. In our culture driven by self-help, we have swallowed an untruth that we can all succeed and live our best lives. Much religion mimics those sentiments, but that is not the truth of life.

For me, Christianity is a religion of uncertainty and ambiguity. It liberates us from certainty and transforms the difficulties of daily existence into the very substance of a journey into the depth of human life. Christian faith has little to do with the debates between theists and nontheists or even atheists. Instead, it helps us confront our brokenness, joyfully embrace the unknown, and courageously face life's difficulties. This transformation creates communities of vulnerability that abandon the false promise of supernatural comfort. Here we can become vulnerable to our own helplessness and face what ails us, not with the intention of finding a remedy, but of better accepting and understanding ourselves. We free ourselves from the chase that often leads us to make choices that in the end cannot and will not deliver on their promises.

I have spent years thinking about a story from the Hebrew Bible (Ezekiel 47) about the prophet Ezekiel, who was led into deep waters by a mysterious figure holding a rope. The movement is oppositional to most theistic positioning—the deeper he went, the less foundation he had. He finally reached a point at which he could no longer touch the bottom of the river, nor could he move against the current. He was drowning.

I often read this story in conjunction with ideas about stages of faith, but lately I have been reading it as a personal story about coming to terms with, as Chödrön says, the ambiguity and the uncertainty of not being able to find footing. Ezekiel has to surrender to his loss of control, and once he is led back to shore, he discovers that the landscape has been dramatically transformed.

What was desert is now alive with lush plant life—echoes of Eden. Perhaps a willingness to relax into ambiguity and uncertainty changes how we see both God and the world.

37

Dead Gods

Beauty in the Wound, collage by me

I have a number of dead gods in my life. They are ideas about the nature of life and its intersection with the divine that once spoke to me but no longer do. Their ghosts linger in the chambers of my heart and haunt me with their old messages. Like my friend, the philosopher Pete Rollins, says, "Most of us don't believe in ghosts, but when something goes bump in the night . . ."

I once heard psychiatrist M. Scott Peck speak at a huge new-age church in Santa Monica. Whereas theologian James Fowler had identified six stages people go through in the journey of faith, Peck had condensed them to four simpler categories in his latest book, *People of the Lie*: chaotic/antisocial, formal/institutional, skeptic/individual, and mystic/communal.

Peck's categories connected with some ideas I had been exploring through a story in the Old Testament about a man and a river, from which I had also derived four stages in a spiritual journey. Turns out, mine were pretty similar: chaos, tradition, doubt, and mystery. As I reflected on the biblical narrative and Peck's categories, I realized they formed the backbone of an exit strategy from theism all together.

The story (Ezekiel 47) goes that Ezekiel, after having a vision, finds himself outside the Temple of the Israelites, where a small trickle of water is beginning to flow eastward. He has been led there by a man—it could have been an angel, could have been God, we don't know. With a measuring rope, this enigmatic figure leads Ezekiel deeper and deeper into a river that materializes in front of them. The story goes through four stages, beginning with the man measuring a thousand cubits (about 1,500 feet) and then finding themselves in ankle-deep water. They move another thousand feet, until the water is knee-deep, then another thousand and the water is to the waist. Finally, after another thousand cubits, they find themselves in water deep enough to swim in and a river that apparently "no one could cross."

This story became my metaphor for religion; it is mobile and flows like a river, rather than stagnant. The idea of chaos is my starting place for religious thinking because I connected the whole notion of coming to water as a place of calm. We speak of dipping our toes into the water to test the temperature, because it has to be just right. To me, that was symbolic of beginning a religious journey—we come to the water's edge and we dip a toe. We hope the waters will bring us something we might be lacking or desiring.

Consider the role of water in nearly all the world's religions. There are holy rivers: the Jordan, the Ganges, the Nile, the Amazon. We ritualize our religions with water: baptisms, cleansings, and healings. "All things live from water," wrote Hafiz, the Sufi poet. So, we come to the water's edge and dip our toes into religion. The water is cool and inviting. Something about it brings a sense of well-being, of order, of our place in the world. I don't think your life needs to be in chaos in order to turn to religion, but I do think we turn to various things in our lives to still the storms that rage in us. Religion is one of them.

The first stage of encountering God is understood as chaos. Going back to the biblical story, the man measures more rope and both he and Ezekiel find themselves up to their ankles in water. "If you wanna touch the sky, you better learn how to kneel," Bono once said—the point is that there has to be some kind of surrender. But the kind of surrender we offer is important. The deeper you go into the waters of religion, the more complicated and dangerous it can become. Knee-high water just might be the most dangerous place of all. I call this the tradition phase, because it is the point at which we can get churched and dangerous. By dangerous, I mean having just enough information to do damage. We often have this nagging human tendency to settle for what's safe, and you have to admit, water at the knees feels nice and safe. You can feel the river's current, but you are submerged only enough that you still remain in control of your body. You're not swimming, but you are no longer in the shallows. Forces are beginning to push against you, but you have yet to encounter uncertainty. Here, at the knees, religion becomes about data, rules, and structure, with clear-cut answers and a place for everything.

For Fowler, this stage is comprised of two phases, the mythic-literal and the synthetic-conventional. In both phases, literalism holds sway, leading to a misunderstanding of symbolic ideas. Conformity is also characteristic of this phase; it gives us a sense of predictability and control. We tend to think human success is connected to control, and with water at our knees, we feel we have mastery over our world. But humans have always been at the mercy of the elements.

Christians are quite willing to say they know something—a lot of things, actually—about God. Tradition tells us much about God that we wouldn't know otherwise, such as the idea that God knows everything, sees everything, is everywhere, and acts without limitation. But placing ourselves in the hands of this omnipresent God is an act of control, not surrender. It's an abdication of the messy business of living, of responsibility for one's own life, which for me is the key message from Jesus.

We have to move, which Ezekiel does quickly as he finds himself up to his waist in water. The currents swirl, threateningly pressing against his body. If you have ever swum in a river, you know this feeling well. From the bank, the water seems gentle, but in the middle of the river you feel vulnerable to the water's power, particularly if you are not a great swimmer. But Ezekiel isn't swimming yet; he is still on his feet in the waist-high water. As he continues deeper into the water, it becomes less benign. He cannot trust the water or himself anymore; he has to start paying attention. A lot happens at this depth. I call this the doubt stage.

Picasso is one of my favorite artists. His work makes me want to create and experiment in my own art and in life, but he is also good for a pithy quote or two. One of my favorites is this little gem: "If you want to preserve tradition, don't wear your grandfather's hat; have grandchildren." The tradition phase is perhaps more like the act of wearing the grandfather's hat; you honor tradition by living in its past glory. You have the effects, but they are not your own; you have not made life, given life, or birthed anything new. For me, tradition is not about preserving the past but fashioning a future from it—having grandchildren if you will. I appreciate tradition because we can discover the best selves we have tried to be before. But I like it with a twist, a healthy dose of the present mixed in.

Perhaps destabilization or deconstruction is a better way to describe the doubt phase, because these are the means by which traditions are made alive again. Doubt disrupts certainty, which comes via the gift of life itself, in this case from the waters Ezekiel found himself wading in. The technical translation of the story says Ezekiel found himself in water up to the loins, the symbolic center of creative life in a past world that understood the body very differently. Things proceeded from the bowels and issued from the loins. The loins brought the seeds of new life; it is also one of the body's most vulnerable parts. Creativity and vulnerability are hallmarks of the doubt phase. When life is destabilized and doubt creeps in, you find yourself feeling confused or vulnerable. Old formulas no longer work, one's power is diminished, and the river's current feels threatening and unsafe.

As the waters rise, we find ourselves further from what we once held sure, more at the mercy of what we don't know than in control of what we do, and still deeper waters call to us. I call this phase mystery. The further one moves away from certainty, the more one moves toward mystery—"the cloud of unknowing," as ancient mystics called it. This is as far as Ezekiel gets in the river, and when he does, his leader asks, "Son of man, do you see this?" It's an admonition to pay attention, surely. But his journey is not over; it's just that the rest of it happens on dry land.

These four stages help decipher the various transitions and changes I have gone through regarding religion and my faith in God. They have framed my questions and liberated me from theological straightjackets I had wrapped myself in—or had allowed others to wrap me in.

But after a time, I realized there was one big issue left: God. Undoubtedly, in the past twenty years or so, there has been a remarkable shift in many Christian circles toward embracing mystery. Rationalist evangelicals have started reading and employing in their services mystical texts and monastic prayers, most of which were born out of an understanding of God as an incomprehensible mystery. I myself feel more comfortable with the idea of the mystical and the unknowable when it comes to the divine. But at the end of the day, we are still thinking about a supernatural, external force that exercises control over human affairs. We can cover that notion with as many veils and as much mystery as we choose, but I still find it problematic for two reasons.

The first is presenting mystery as the ultimate stage of religious experience. Embracing the mystical conception of the sacred is often viewed as some kind of achievement, whether it be Zen, enlightenment, salvation, or inner peace. The second reason is that Ezekiel is still led back to shore after swimming with the man with the measuring cord. While they were in the water, the land transformed from dry desert to a blossoming, Eden-like state. This led me to consider a fifth stage in which my religious life takes place not in the holy waters of God, but in the aftermath of that. In presenting spiritual life as a staged event, it essentially becomes about whether one still believes certain things they used to. You once thought God was omnipotent, but now you don't. You used to refer to God in the masculine, now you don't. You come to some new position for which you need new propositions, ideas, and expressions. Ezekiel finds himself back on dry land that's laid out before him like the garden of Eden. It is a new material world in which all kinds of fruitful things have come to life. I call this the post-mystical world, but perhaps it is simply a different kind of mysticism. It is the kind that frees you from distrusting the world, the kind that doesn't swim in the river of God but revels in the beauty of life, the kind firmly rooted in the "dust of this planet," as Eugene Thacker describes it.

Some have called Ezekiel a prophet of hope. He spoke of restoring much of what Israel had lost in his time, and he envisioned a world with a renewed lease on life. But that life is marked by its unpredictability, destabilization, and disruption of the normal flow of things. It resists being cataloged, labeled, and confined by conventional wisdom and prevailing trends.

38

Hello, Darkness

Every revelation partook more of significant darkness than of
explanatory light.

—Herman Melville, *Moby Dick*

I am fascinated by the idea of darkness—shadows, within and
without, places characterized by the absence of light. My taste
might have developed in reaction to being in religious environs
fixated on light and the eradication of darkness.

It emerged from a number of sources, really. One was a piece
of art that put me in touch with a theological concept I had
overlooked for a long time. Years ago, I visited an exhibit called
"The Genius of Rome" at the Royal Academy of Arts in London. The exhibit explored the Italian Renaissance painter Caravaggio, one of my favorite artists, and his influence on other
painters. Caravaggio is viewed as a refiner of chiaroscuro, an
artistic process that uses strong tonal contrast between light and
dark to incredible effect. The idea of the time was that forms
are best expressed when light falls onto them, so paintings of
his time always use strong sources of light. Shadows always sur-
round the subjects in his paintings, creating a sense of claustro-
phobia that I admire. Exuding life and energy, his works feel as

though you could hide in their shadows as a bystander in whatever scene is depicted.

Struck by the Caravaggio exhibit, I pursued my own research on the artist and came across his painting *The Conversion of Saint Paul*, which is set in a church in Rome. In the scene—Catholically anecdotal and apocryphal as it is—Paul has fallen from his horse. Let's call that artistic license, because it's not in the actual biblical text, which is a key difference between Catholic and Protestant portrayals of scriptural events. Protestant portrayals of this scene tend to ignore the horse, often going for literalism or avoiding the visual arts completely. But Caravaggio's painting so moved me that it sent me back to a text in the Bible I had felt pretty familiar with. Of course, once I came to it again, I saw something I hadn't noticed before.

Paul's conversion is most often presented in terms of light by those who speak for God. After all, that's how we tend to present our religious conversions: we come to the light, things are enlightened or revealed, and scales fall from our eyes. But in the story of Paul's conversion, he is struck blind first. The conversion begins with three days of darkness—symbolic and Christic. I hadn't noticed that before. Something about this blindness appealed to me. It is an internal movement, and Paul is completely shut off from everything and rendered immobile. This man who had been furiously running around, attempting to stifle an upstart and heretical movement, is suddenly incapacitated to the point where he has to be led around by the hand.

The scales don't fall from his eyes when he has this encounter with Jesus; instead, his eyes become scaled, and the blindness becomes a pathway to a new understanding about himself and about life. Blindness and sight, lightness and darkness, are not opposites. Rather, they are coconspirators working to bring us into contact with the mysteries and depths of existence. For Paul, insight came at the "cost" of blindness, an idea I picked up from the writer Paul de Man in his 1971 book *Blindness and*

Insight. It's similar to Blind Bartimaeus in the gospels, whose capacity to see Jesus comes from his blindness—unlike the Pharisees, whom Jesus labels blind guides, even though they can see quite well, except that they can't see him. They are blinded by their preconditioned fixed position that he couldn't possibly be a prophet because he was a Galilean, a carpenter's son, or whatever other bias precluded them from truly seeing.

We all have blindness. We all only see, for the most part, what we want to see. I would argue that most of us are blinded by our prejudices and biases to the true nature of reality, much like the Pharisees. We think we see clearly, but we don't see that well at all. We do theology from our blind spots, from a fixed position outside of the text, then we avoid the bits that don't conform to our notions of the way things are. This is how people get the Scriptures to say what they want them to. You don't believe in drinking? Then you can go with a Scripture from Ephesians 5:18, "Do not be drunk with wine, wherein is excess." You fancy a drink? Then head straight to Proverbs 31:7 "Let the poor get drunk to forget his troubles." There is a Bible verse for every blind spot of our own fixed positions. Morality binds us and blinds us.

This, to me, is the manner of Paul's conversion. He cannot turn away; however, his hand is forced by the very act of being struck blind. I also believe the story is symbolic. Whether it happened doesn't interest me. What it opens up for my life is what captivates me.

Moving toward God might ultimately be a move toward the depth of oneself. This might be too anthropocentric of an interpretation of the religious equation. Still, I find the journey of human life toward a better understanding of place and function to be more compelling than thinking about a metaphysical other (God) with whom we are supposed to connect. This is how religion functions for me these days.

My views on religion have changed dramatically over the

years. I began with fairly conservative views. Or, let me say, I was given a conservative form of religion, which was presented to me as complete truth, and I tried for some time to live into its demands and invitations.

It didn't take long for it to fail me or for me to fail it, but it took me a while to address that failing. The failing of that particular form of religion, that initial collapse, was perhaps more of an expansion, really. I was forced to walk away or to dig deeper. It taught me an invaluable lesson: to stand still is to fall backward. It also taught me that there is no light without darkness. I was offered a certain light, but it was without shadow. Everything was presented as plain and simple and clear. I was in the light, except I wasn't. The thing that was lacking was an exposure to the dark. I don't mean dark in a demonic or evil sense; I mean the darkness of uncertainty, obscurity, the unseeable. Paul was plunged into darkness and out of this he emerged into a future he could never have envisioned in the light. As Virginia Woolf once wrote in her diary, "The future is dark, which is the best thing the future can be" (*The Diary of Virginia Woolf: 1915-1919*). I have learned to prize the dark—the uncertain, the unseeable, the unknowable—and to find a different kind of comfort from it.

Beliefs, like everything else in the modern world, need to be revisited. We no longer live static, fixed medieval existences in which everything is held in place by the great chain of being. We have exchanged stasis for fluidity, a sense of being somewhere for being everywhere, and a fixed identity for multiple selves and dress-up and play.

39

Losing Jesus

Triple XXX, collage by me

When I first started exploring religion, I was looking for clues that pointed toward things I felt I were missing in my life, or at least things I didn't have sorted out and wanted to change. I thought Christianity might offer those clues, but ultimately it got in the way. Christianity, or the form of Christianity I was exposed to, was an all-encompassing system of belief. I embraced it for a while, though it never felt quite right.

I had been on the road with AC/DC for a few years around then, so I had saved enough money to live on without working. So having decided that a change was necessary and with all that extra time on my hands, I left the world of rock and roll and embarked on another leg of life's journey. I became involved in a church. It was nondenominational, formed out of the Calvary Chapel and Vineyard Churches that littered Southern California. Products of the 1960s counterculture, those churches' understanding of Jesus had emerged from the ashes of hippie idealism. In spite of rejecting institutional religions as relics of a bygone age, 1960s youths didn't exclude spirituality from their searches for new ways of life. While the mainstream church and many radical theologians of the time declared God was dead, a spiritual revolution was underway in youth culture in the image of a long-haired revolutionary Jesus preaching love and good works. They may have rejected organized religion, but "Jesus Is Just Alright," as the Doobie Brothers declared in 1966.

The slow divide between religion and spirituality began in the 1960s, as new churches formed that preached a more spiritual Jesus of relationship, community, love, and grace. These churches were not mainstream; their message was new and countercultural. But their hippie idealism was married with a more conservative theological perspective that emphasized sin, dark understandings of the world, and human nature. People were accepted as part of the new tribe as long as they were ready to leave the past firmly behind and get a new life with Jesus.

Post-AC/DC, the first cracks in my new religious armor came

through music. I was still linked to my musical past through some of my Los Angeles Christian friends, who played in a band and had a deal with a Christian record company. We sang and wrote songs together, but it was hardly rock 'n' roll. Their Beatles-esque sound got them a bit of a following and a fair amount of trouble with some church leaders, who thought them too worldly and devilish. At the time, in the early 1980s, feelings ran high about secular society and the dangers of popular culture—particularly pop music's demonic nature.

Disillusioned by our experiences, my friends and I began to wonder what was really going on under this veneer of supposedly cool religiosity. We had been raised on pop music, so letting it go was not an option. I quickly realized that many Christian leaders had done little critical thinking about culture and what was really going on in society. Things were reduced to pietistic and outdated mentalities of us versus them, the sacred/secular divide. But these were the people who were supposedly collapsing those divides and blurring the lines! The very Jesus they were worshipping had been given to them by the youth culture. Yet here they were, trashing it and declaring it devoid of any goodness.

I tried to focus on the positives. I voraciously read philosophy, theology, and sociology. I was at the church every time the doors opened. In a church like this, leadership was an open opportunity conferred upon people on the basis of friendship, preference, and access to networks. I was well liked and eager to contribute, so I rose through the community's ranks.

Once, I was asked to speak at a Wednesday meeting. I'd never before spoken in public—I was unbelievably shy—but for some reason I agreed and found myself not the least bit nervous. And I did well. I discovered that it was easy to speak in a public setting—much easier than in the intimacy of real life. Before long, I was the center of it all. I was appointed to leadership and my life became the business of professional Christian ministry: preaching, teaching, and running a church. This was something I had never desired or imagined, but it just sort of happened.

I still felt uneasy about the church, but I continued to push that feeling down. For a while, the newness and the learning curve of everything distracted me from my nagging doubts. I forced myself into ways of thinking and living that I was told were good and right, but eventually I grew to hate myself for my internal resistance to my new world. I figured the problem was me. That's the tyranny of self-doubt: you seldom give yourself the credit for what you think and feel. It's a heavy weight to carry, and carry it I did.

It's funny how something small can come along and, in a moment, entirely undo your life. A word spoken in passing, an unexpected situation, someone you meet, a movie you watch—it can pull back the curtain on your existence and expose the fragility of what you are trying to hold together. I was getting lost in religion—lost in the business of church, and not in a good way. I was surrounded by people who saw the world as a dark and dangerous place full of temptations and godlessness, but I did not see the world the way they did. I did not fear the world that way. For all my melancholy, I really like life—the gritty realities of living. I also have little problem with people whose lives don't follow the same pathway as mine—that's what makes things interesting. Homogeneity has never appealed to me. But I was feeling the pressure of these peoples' expectations, their assumptions about how I should look, act, and think.

I was living in the world of shoulds. "God commands . . ." "Jesus wants you to do this and not that," "Paul says . . ." It was all wearing on me. I was trying to live up to something that was beyond me, and I slowly realized I didn't believe much of what I was being told, or even what I was saying myself. I was trying to be faithful to the community and the powers that be, but I didn't agree with their perspectives. The more I read, the more I realized there many other ways to think.

During this critical juncture in my life—a time when I was looking for something, anything, to guide me through whatever lay ahead—three things came in quick succession that set me on a new path: a line of Scripture, an idea in a book, and a cassette tape.

The line of Scripture came from the story in the Gospel of Luke in which Mary, Joseph, and Jesus joined other pilgrims to celebrate the Passover festival in Jerusalem. After it ended and they all headed home, the text reads nonchalantly, "The boy Jesus stayed behind in Jerusalem, but they were unaware of it. Thinking he was in their company, they traveled on for a day" (Luke 2:43–44). It's a simple recounting of an ancient story, one I had read many times before, but this time it jumped out at me. They had lost Jesus in Jerusalem, then went back to look for him. That's *exactly* how I felt. Here I was, up to my neck in the business of the church, but I felt distanced from the very thing that had brought me there in the first place.

Organized Christianity sometimes makes much more of Paul than it does of Jesus. Of course, Jesus gets honorable mention—he's hard to ignore completely—but most of the time, conversations about what the church should be become an investigation of Paul's views on the topic. I missed Jesus and had a gnawing sense that I needed to recover something central to me about how all this religious stuff I had found myself wrapped up in fit with who I wanted to be. As clueless as I was, I didn't quit—and I still haven't. I'm not sure why.

Around the time I had this epiphany with the story in Luke, I came across a quote from Einstein that said, "Every man must strive to be a voice and not an echo." There it was: another little clue. There was something uniquely for me in that invocation—encouragement to find my own voice, speak my own truth, and not simply repeat what others say. The clue to being yourself is to own your thoughts and feelings, to work out your true beliefs, even if they contradict conventional wisdom.

Finding your voice can take a lifetime. Perhaps it begins in emulation or imitation; we tend to model ourselves on those we value. It's like being in a band. You start by learning the songs of your musical idols, building up enough skill until you dare to think you could write a song too. That's the day you come into your own as musician and start to define your own particular sound and feel. I understood the process when it came to music; I hadn't thought it was the same for the rest of life. I wasn't sure how to begin, but I sure as shit wanted to try.

Maybe a month or a year later, a friend gave me a cassette tape. It was a recording of a talk on Christian leadership, a topic I was less than enthusiastic about at the time. But it was from a speaker outside the circles I moved in and my friend recommended it, so I gave it a chance. It began: "The task of the Christian leader . . . is to guard the great questions." That's about as far as I got. I have no idea what else that tape said, but those words have been indelibly inscribed on my heart ever since. *Guard the great questions.* That's not an earth-shattering idea, you might be thinking. And you are right. But I had immersed myself in an understanding of Christianity that had no interest in questions, only answers. God had answers for everything. All you needed to know about God, yourself, the world, and others could be found in the Bible and modeled in the narratives of Jesus. Questions don't need to be guarded; just find the answers and everything will slide into place. But this reminder—to cherish and guard the questions that make up our faith, lives, and very existences—shook me. What if you don't ask the right questions, or even know what they are? What *are* the great questions? I didn't know.

The speaker was referring to the questions of ultimate meaning—the dilemma of the human condition, the trauma of life—that constantly arise in the human psyche. But I took those words and personalized them. What are the great questions *I* am asking of the world, of life, of God? "Listen to your life," wrote theologian Frederick Buechner. "See it for the fathomless mystery it is." I hadn't been listening to my life. Well, I might have been listening, but certainly had not been paying attention. Until now.

This quickly became the basic framework for a new direction in my life down a bumpy road out of particular forms of Christian faith. Since the late 1980s and early '90s, those three kernels of ideas have shaped my life.

So, I left that church. I've since left a couple more, some of them well and others not so well. But this one I left by moving away, and I started another with a group of friends. Well, it wasn't a church—I started a project that has been ongoing for the last couple decades. It's built around finding other ways of thinking and practicing religion, searching instead for religionless forms of faith and post-theistic expressions of religion.

One of the first things I did after leaving was commit to a theological education. I decided to explore the questions that interested me, so I could research and reflect on all the aspects of religion and theology I wanted to investigate. I went to seminary—not because I wanted a degree, but for access to information and ideas beyond my reach.

I arrived at seminary armed with questions and a whole load of answers I had been given that I knew didn't work for me. I set about the long process of refining my interests down to their core and reframing what I thought about life, God, and religion. The questions I guard are held between the folds of those three elements. I threw away old maps and set out to chart new ones. You can get lost without a map, but getting lost is the beginning of learning; it's how you create new maps.

At seminary, I wanted to explore the new cultural contexts that religion and Christianity found themselves in. I wanted to better understand this new deterritorialized world of late twentieth-century life in which the old theological codes no longer worked. This world was shaped by popular culture, by technology that has reframed our sense of self in relation to others and to the sacred; learning about religion means learning about the culture from which it came. French feminist philosopher Julia Kristeva, in her 2006 book *This Incredible Need Believe*, named our new context of belief as the dichotomy between the "need to believe" and the "desire to know." Both are driven by a hunger to make meaning in our lives amidst the reality of a world filled with new knowledge, emerging complex science, and ideas that challenge our age-old views. Everyone is a skeptic, and we are all atheists at least once a day, even if we say we believe in God.

So, I set out on this new adventure of discovery not knowing where I was headed, but with a hunger to recover what I had lost and to discover other things about myself, life, belief, and God. I wanted to reconcile my various interests: music, art, culture, theology, philosophy, religion, belief. My interest in philosophy, Camus's notion of the absurd, Jean-François Lyotard's rejection of meta-narrative, Nietzsche's nihilism—all these ideas that fired my curiosity and passion—how could they fit together? Were there ways of thinking about religion that felt more cohesive to me? Could a community be shaped out of nonbelief, out of brokenness? Could a space be created in which people weren't fixed but accepted? Could space be made for doubt, atheism, or a/theism?

I wanted to examine what the writer Fernando Pessoa called the "sickness of the eyes": that dullness born of familiarity, the tacit acceptance of the way things are. His remedy for this was poetry. Poetry was his process of unlearning. Poets reminds us what we already know and interpret what we already understand. Jesus was my poet; he helped me in the process of unlearning, addressing the sickness of my eyes and inviting me to cultivate a sense of the world around me. That was what I liked about Jesus, his "this-worldliness." For him, there was no escape from life, there was no need for any way out. What we need is a way in, a way to get deeper into life. Jesus was the poet who came to heal the sickness of our eyes by telling us what we already knew. "You have heard it said, but I say unto you," he said (Matt 5:27–28). He was pointing to what was right under our noses so that we could see again. I wanted to see again. I want to see.

40

Notes on the Death of God

For more than thirty years, I have spoken with great regularity and increasing uncertainty about God. I talk about God, but I am not sure I have ever truly believed in God conceptually; God just came with the territory alongside other things I really believed in. But finally, I am at a stage in life where I find the uncertainty about such things to be truly liberating; it serves as a springboard from which to speak about things I do not know that have yet shaped my life. Only when we lose certainty can we come close to experiencing a sense of the sacred.

I carry snippets of ideas around with me like receipts in my pockets. Occasionally, I take them out, unfold their crumpled edges, and smooth them out. I read and reflect upon them, then I toss away some and tuck others back in the pocket of my heart, where they will live for a while longer. I want to read them again later.

I have lived long enough to realize that all too often we predict the demise of things much too early—rock 'n' roll is dead, books are dead, hip-hop is dead, fashion is dead, God is dead. In every case, that declaration was at once true and premature. Certain aspects of those things were assigned to the grave and eclipsed by the march of time, technology, or desire. At the same time, all those things declared dead indeed live on, whether undead or alive, but definitely not the same.

Take God, for example. The death of God has as much to do with shifting conceptions of the sacred than God's ultimate disappearance or irrelevance. It is about the drying up of a particular meaning, a shift in how humans perceive their world, and as such, what might lie beyond or behind it. What is at stake is not a question of theism versus atheism.

Today, the death of God is really a conversation about the death of the death of God, or living with God in the aftermath of his death. It is about the relationship between the iconic and the idolatrous. The philosopher Jean-Luc Nancy has said that Christianity is not a normal religion, but the religion of the exit from religion. As such, its task is to make religion as idolatry disappear.

God's Tombstone, iPad sketch by me

41

Religion and a Rabbit's Foot

I have been thinking a lot this past year. For a long time, I have been restless, frustrated, angry, despairing, and sometimes hopeful, but mostly not. I find most experiences of religion, whether in my pastoral role or my academic one, to be predictable and uninteresting. Part of me feels it is not worth the inner turmoil and I should simply walk away, but then what?

Until I answer that equation, I shall remain in a state of inner conflict. I am torn between taking a wild leap into the dark and working out what moves are available to me. I can't find my way to either place at the moment, so I shall try to make my frustrations work for me. I am still interested in all my basic questions about God, religion, life, and faith, but I am interested in religion in the places where it is least obvious. I sometimes feel religion exists in a cycle of self-understanding from which it will never free itself and I will always be at odds with it. It is not all bad—in fact, some of it is great; I just need to figure out how to work within it in a way that is healthy and life-giving to me and to my community.

Religion is difficult to wrestle with, something demonstrated in the etymology of the word. The dictionary is vague on the origin of the word religion. It is often declared—usually by religious people—to be derived from the Latin *religare*, "to bind"—which fits nicely with the idea of God and religion inextricably interwoven. But others say it evolved from *relegere*, which means "to reread." These two stems could lead to quite different understandings of what exactly is going on when we talk about religion. Perhaps religion is best understood as having a couple different trajectories. But if those trajectories aren't held in tension, you get a form of religion that has no bite and resists change. "The last experience of God is often the obstacle to the next experience of God," Richard Rohr once said at a conference I hosted with some friends.

My tension lies in the fact that we are in a time of upheaval and destabilization, and I am often in environments where the response to that is to avoid the problem rather than rise to meet it head-on. During my doctoral work, I studied sociologist Pitirim Sorokin's theory about cultural development, which classified societies according to what he termed their "cultural mentality." Societies can be "ideational" (reality is spiritual), "sensate" (reality is material), or "idealistic" (a synthesis of the two). He suggested that major civilizations evolve from an ideational to an idealistic mentality, then eventually to a sensate one. Each phase of cultural development not only describes the nature of reality, but also stipulates the nature of human needs and goals to be satisfied, the extent to which they should be satisfied, and their methods of satisfaction. Sorokin's theory was controversial and flawed, but I was taken by the fact that many of his theoretical prognoses were born out of studying literature and the arts as much as economics and other indicators.

Using Sorokin's theory, we might say we are transitioning from an ideational period into a sensate one, blending our materialism with spirituality, although we don't operate with such distinct binaries these days. That shift destabilizes religion, and this is what interests me.

Lots of religious talk seeks to offer stabilization and security, maintaining the idea that religion is a talismanic set of beliefs about the world, like a rabbit's foot. For me, religion, and Christian faith in particular, is not a set of beliefs. Instead, it is an expression of a way of being in the world, embracing the world in order to discover life.

42

Apocalypse Will Blossom

At the 2018 Grammy Awards, female artists wore white roses as a sign of solidarity with the Time's Up initiative against sexual harassment and assault in the entertainment industry. With one exception: Lorde, whose album *Melodrama* had been nominated for Album of the Year, wore a striking scarlet Valentino gown. To the back of the dress, Lorde had hand-stitched a piece of paper with a poem by the artist Jenny Holzer.

Holzer began her career as a painter, but in the 1970s she abandoned that style in an effort to reach and connect more directly with a broader audience. As an abstract artist, she found meaning in the concepts art expresses, rather than in its form. Taking language as her material, she created a series of posters called *Inflammatory Essays* and posted them around New York City from 1979 to 1982. Each poster was printed on colored paper and contained exactly one hundred words of text. These inflammatory essays were exactly that: carefully crafted and confrontational meditations drawing from thinkers in the communist and anarchistic traditions, such as Vladimir Lenin, Mao Zedong, Karl Marx, and Friedrich Engels. The posters addressed issues such as violence, consumerism, interpersonal relationships, and abuses of power.

From this series, Lorde had chosen "The Apocalypse Will Blossom" for her dress, declaring it online, "My version of a white rose." The piece begins with the Psalmic admonition, "Rejoice!", but immediately declares that we should do so because the times we live in are intolerable. The piece calls for a revolutionary overthrow of power and ends provocatively with the words, "The apocalypse will blossom." The apocalypse is a revealing, a disclosure of knowledge, or an impartation of revelation. In our time, it has largely negative connotations—perhaps because we always resist the intrusion of upheaval—but an apocalypse is a creative deconstruction and a dismantling of the old world that then reveals a new one. In its essence, the apocalypse encourages the metamorphosis of society. Lorde wore the poem as an act of solidarity, but also as an invitation to participate in this upheaval. Wearing a rose is not enough in the face of abused power, injustice, racism, or bigotry. Real action must be taken, and Lorde was issuing a call to arms.

How does an apocalypse blossom? How are new worlds made possible? Italian philosopher Franco "Bifo" Berardi says there are two kinds of apocalypses: negative and positive. When a society enters a crisis stage, things begin collapsing and we experience the negative apocalypse. What once held us no longer supports us, what once stabilized us now feels unstable. But at the same time, we can glimpse the horizon of possibility, which is how he describes a positive apocalypse. This notion applies to many of the institutions that once gave our lives stability and consistency. No part of life isn't in a state of flux, whether it's economics, politics, sexuality, or gender—everywhere we turn, we see things crumbling, worlds collapsing, and old ways no longer working as they once did. That's true in Christianity as well. So much is moving, and people are seeking ways to navigate new worlds of understanding about faith. "All things that have form eventually decay," said the Japanese artist Masashi Kishimoto, but we always seem surprised when they do.

Religion and Christianity have long provided a sense of harmony and order to the chaotic human existence. They have offered meaning and given shape to the experience of being human by addressing our craving for order, our desire for purpose. I have given up on that view of religion and the gods that go with it. If Christian faith is essentially believing certain things about a supernatural God and surrendering to a magical thinking about reality, then I no longer have faith. If Christian faith is about a way of being and a posture toward reality that sees it for what it is, then maybe I still have some.

In his 1989 book *Contingency, Irony, and Solidarity*, Richard Rorty wrote about the contingence of language. He says what makes interesting philosophy is seldom wrestling with the opposing ideas of a particular thesis. This wrestling sounds characteristic of our interactions in the world today—people of polarized thought throwing their arguments at each other to prove themselves right and their opposers wrong. What makes it interesting, Rorty says, is the contest between an "entrenched vocabulary which has become a nuisance and a half-formed new vocabulary which vaguely promises great things." History shows us, he says, that the instrument for cultural change is not argument but instead a "talent for speaking differently" about things. If we want change, we not only have to ignore the traditional questions and answers, but replace them with new ones. Certain ways of speaking make certain questions possible, but those may not be the questions we need to ask today.

So, this is where I find myself these days: living with the end of meaning and the end of God, and with a desire to be an opening for and to life in the world.

For your listening pleasure

1. Donnie Hathaway: Extensions of A Man
2. Stevie Wonder: Music of My Mind
3. Nina Simone: Baltimore
4. Sam Cooke: The Best of Sam Cooke
5. Dennis Brown: No Man Is An Island
6. Sex Pistols: Nevermind the Bollocks
7. P.J. Harvey: Let England Shake
8. Joseph Arthur: Redemption's Son
9. Iggy Pop: Post Pop Depression
10. Nick Cave: Push the Sky Away
11. AC/DC: Dirty Deeds Done Dirt Cheap

OR → Anything by Bowie ★

A playlist to read by, iPad sketch by me

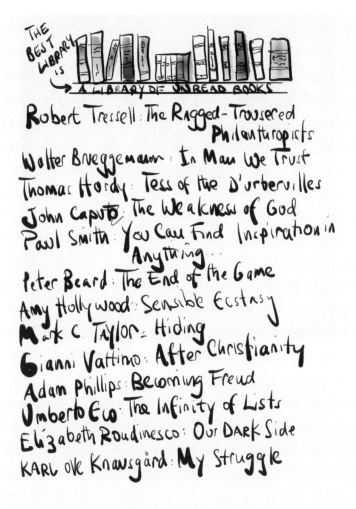

THE BEST LIBRARY IS → A LIBRARY OF UNREAD BOOKS

Robert Tressell: The Ragged-Trousered Philanthropists
Walter Brueggemann: In Man We Trust
Thomas Hardy: Tess of the D'urbervilles
John Caputo: The Weakness of God
Paul Smith: You Can Find Inspiration in Anything...
Peter Beard: The End of the Game
Amy Hollywood: Sensible Ecstasy
Mark C. Taylor: Hiding
Gianni Vattimo: After Christianity
Adam Phillips: Becoming Freud
Umberto Eco: The Infinity of Lists
Elizabeth Roudinesco: Our Dark Side
Karl Ove Knausgård: My Struggle

A Library of Unread Books, iPad sketch by me

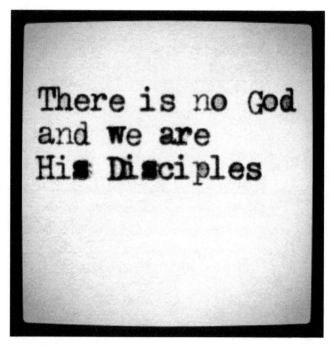

Quote by me, iPad sketch by me

Self-portrait collage by me